D1486257

30131 05804113 5

I Am Norwell Roberts

I Am Norwell Roberts

The story of the Met's first Black police officer

NORWELL ROBERTS

First published in Great Britain in 2022 by Two Roads
An Imprint of John Murray Press
An Hachette UK company

1

Copyright © Revelation Films Ltd 2022

A CIP catalogue record for this title is available from the British Library

Hardback ISBN 978 1 399 80088 4
eBook ISBN 978 1 399 80090 7

Typeset in Bembo MT by Hewer Text UK Ltd, Edinburgh
Printed and bound in Great Britain by Clays Ltd, Elcograf S.p.A.

John Murray policy is to use papers that are natural, renewable and
recyclable products and made from wood grown in sustainable forests.
The logging and manufacturing processes are expected to conform
to the environmental regulations of the country of origin.

Two Roads
Carmelite House
50 Victoria Embankment
London EC4Y 0DZ

www.tworoadsbooks.com

This book is for all those people who believed in me and hoped I would prove the doubters wrong.

'To appreciate the present and how far we have come, we sometimes need to revisit the uncomfortable past, no matter how painful.'

Norwell Roberts QPM

Contents

Preface

IT WAS THE morning of 10 July 1967, a bright and sunny day, and I arrived at Bow Street Police Station in the West End of London, a smartly dressed twenty-two-year-old police officer with butterflies in my stomach. A few months earlier, I'd become the first Black recruit to the Metropolitan Police Force, the culmination of a long-held ambition, and since then I'd completed a sixteen-week training course. I'd never felt so proud – I was so excited about my new career. But as soon as I'd been introduced to my reporting sergeant, the air in his office seemed to sour and he greeted me with a snarl. 'Look, you nigger, I'll see to it that you won't finish your probation,' he said. No one stood up for me – the officers who were in the room looked the other way, and I thought I could see a few of them smirking behind their hands. I'd never thought being London's first Black police officer was going to be easy, but nothing had prepared me for the difficulties that lay ahead.

What you are about to read is completely true – some names have been omitted to protect the guilty, but that's all – everything else is my story, just as it happened. However, my aim isn't to make people feel sorry for me; all I want is to describe how things were, to take you back to the 'bad old days', so that we can learn from them. You may well ask why I'm so special. The answer is I'm not – I was just lucky enough to be in the right place at the right time.

It might seem unlikely now, but for a long time the 'Old Bill' was completely white, with absolutely nothing in the way of ethnic diversity. That meant that when I joined in 1967, I was the only Black officer in a force of over 27,000. Being the first at anything is always tricky, but the first individuals to climb Everest, to run the four-minute mile or to land on the moon had the support of their peers. Being the first Black policeman might not seem quite so dramatic as those achievements, but at least Sir Edmund Hilary and Tenzing Norgay could give each other a helpful shove! My situation was very different – in fact, it often felt like the entire Metropolitan Police Force was pushing me in the opposite direction, willing me to fail.

I had some experience of being 'the first' even before I joined the police force – I was the first Black boy at my primary school and at the first secondary school I attended. From school, I went to work as a laboratory technician, and it was only after I'd been in that job for five years or so that I was struck by an overwhelming urge to become a policeman.

If I wanted to be philosophical, I suppose I could say that my experiences with discrimination helped me learn what I was capable of. After a long career in the police force, not to mention a childhood in which I suffered a good deal of racial discrimination, I can honestly say that I bear no malice to any of the people who treated me badly. I do, however, have one or two scars. The most visible one is on my forehead, and I've had it since I was twelve, when a bunch of fifth formers at my school in Bromley in Kent, who were much bigger than me, dropped me on my head, curious to discover the colour of my blood. To this day, it shocks me that they were amazed to find out it was red, just like theirs.

I'm pretty sure that other Black men had applied to join the Met before I did, but none of them had been successful. For reasons only known to the Home Secretary, my application made it through, and I was in – the Metropolitan Police finally had its first Black policeman. What followed was a thirty-year career of incredible highs and some pretty shitty lows, and there were plenty of times when things were so tough that I found it hard to keep going. I can still remember how often I felt like giving it all up to do something else. But through all of it, what made me carry on was the thought that I had something to prove. I wanted to succeed even more than other people wanted me to fail!

Things eventually went full circle – the blokes who had sworn that they would never speak to me when I first joined the force would come up to me after work and ask if they could buy me a drink. In fact, some of the people who gave me the most stick to start with have since decided that they want to be friends with me. I loved the job and fought hard to become accepted on my merits and performance – for me, the colour of my skin had nothing to do with it. I guess that, eventually, everyone realised that my blood was red – just like theirs.

I experienced some shocking treatment from within the police force. I was staggered by some of the things I had to put up with; the early years of my police career were a steep learning curve. But I have no doubt that these things would have happened to whoever was the first Black policeman in the Metropolitan Police Force; in spite of everything, I'm glad it was me and I have no regrets.

Looking back on what happened with the benefit of hindsight, I could never have resigned. After all, if I had not made a success of my police career, other Black people might have been put off joining. It was clear to me that I had to set a good example – if I messed things up, my detractors would have been able to say, 'You see – we tried and it didn't work. We don't need them.'

Despite the discrimination that many Black police officers have suffered over the years, the police force has long struggled to admit that it is institutionally racist; in most cases the unacceptable behaviour is so deeply entrenched that the powers that be are genuinely unable to see it – or perhaps they don't want to. Of course, there's also the fact that if they don't accept that something's wrong, they don't have to do anything to correct it – but this means that things will never get better.

The easy option, of course, is to do nothing, for fear of 'rocking the boat', but it's important that we fight for change. I was one of the police officers who was instrumental in turning the Black Police Association from an idea into a reality, and it's change like this that means that I would now encourage anybody to join the police force. We need male and female police officers of all colours and from all cultures – it's crucial that the people who are protecting us reflect our multiracial society. I continue to provide a sympathetic ear to any Black and Asian officers who want advice. In fact, if any officer of any ethnicity whatsoever is having trouble, they can always talk to me. I love the idea that I still set an example to others – I always hope they think, *Well, if Norwell Roberts made it all those years ago, so can I!*

In an interview I gave to the *Big Issue* in 1996, I said that I was looking forward to my retirement the following year. After thirty years in the force, I said I couldn't wait for the day when I had the option of getting out of bed in the morning, looking out the window and thinking, *No, forget it*, and going back to bed. I added, 'I might just write a book.' Well, twenty-five years after I retired, I finally have.

I

Anguilla

I WAS BORN ON the island of Anguilla on Tuesday, 23 October 1945, just a few months after the end of the Second World War, and was christened Norwell Lionel Gumbs. Anguilla is, to this day, a British Overseas Territory in what used to be called the British West Indies. Its name is believed to have been given to it by the explorer Christopher Columbus, and comes from the Italian word for eel, in reference to the island's long, thin shape.

I grew up in Anguilla's capital, The Valley, which is a small town in the centre of the island. Anguilla would make the news in the late sixties, when there was a bit of an uprising against it being under the control of St Kitts and Nevis. On 30 May 1967, a crowd of local people ejected the St Kitts and Nevis Police Force; following a referendum, they declared themselves independent in what became known as the Anguilla Revolution. Interestingly, it was never about gaining independence from Britain – the population seemed perfectly happy with that!

In 1969, 300 Metropolitan Police officers were sent to the island to help the locals maintain the peace. I often wonder what would have happened if I'd been one of those people selected to return to the island of my birth to help stabilise it. I can only suppose that I was not experienced enough to be chosen – I was just two years into my police career, after all – but it now seems clear to me that my presence might have helped. In any case, the island is thankfully politically stable now, and it has enjoyed a large growth in tourism and offshore finance.

Gumbs was my dad's surname, and the name I grew up with. In 1968, a year after I'd become London's first Black police officer, I changed it by deed poll to Roberts, my mother's maiden name. The main reason for the change was quite straightforward: I was attracting a lot of publicity and the press just kept misspelling my name, in a variety of different ways. I was called 'Gumms', 'Gums', 'Gumps' and even 'Gomes'. Compared to all those incorrect options, Roberts seemed much simpler. From 1968, I was able to sign official documents as Norwell Roberts. I've got used to it in the decades since then.

I grew up in a small house with my mother and her parents. We owned a fair amount of land, both around the house and elsewhere – I suppose it could be called a smallholding. We used to grow fresh vegetables and kept cows, hens, sheep and goats – which meant a constant supply of milk and eggs – and the house had a large cistern outside that collected the rainwater. Everyone in the community had a piece of land that belonged to them, though I've no idea how it was worked out – it must have gone back generations.

Anguilla was a small island, and everyone seemed to be related. There were lots of people who I thought of as cousins, uncles or aunties, but it was hard to know whether I was actually related to them or if they were family friends. In the community I grew up in, there were no telephones, but you didn't need them – everyone knew each other, and news spread by word of mouth. There was only one doctor, one hospital and one dentist.

I don't have any childhood memories of my dad – he was only around for the first few years of my life. I don't have any photos of myself as a child, and nor do I have any of my parents during our time in Anguilla. As far as I can remember, no one had a camera. It makes me a bit sad, but I guess it's just one of those things.

I was always led to believe that my dad died when I was three, so when I learned many years later that he had actually moved to

America, it came as a complete surprise. I now understand that he remarried and had several children, but I don't know much more than that – some threads of life are best left unpulled. His name was Everard Gumbs, and he was known as 'Ebby'. I gather that he had gone to the US Virgin Islands to help with the war effort in the early 1940s, before returning to Anguilla in 1944. He was a fisherman, the same as his father, and he lived with his elderly mother, who I called 'Grandma'. I still remember going out into the ocean with my grandad as a very little boy and fishing from his rowing boat. I used to help him to pull in his fishing pots and we'd examine what we'd caught together.

As for my mother, her name was Georgina. I don't know what she did for a living in those days, but she certainly worked. I believe she was born in 1922, so she would have been in her early twenties when I was born and her early thirties when she came to England. She married the man who became my step-father in around 1960, when we were living in the UK, but he proved to be abusive and she was granted a divorce. I can still remember giving evidence in her favour during the divorce hearing at Clerkenwell Magistrates' Court, the building I would regularly attend many years later to see the criminals I had arrested appear in court.

The only photograph that I have of my mother hangs in my study at home. She's smiling in the picture, even though she was very ill when it was taken, in the first few years of this century. The only thing I do not like about it is that she was wearing what we called a 'syrup' – rhyming slang for wig (a 'syrup of fig'). I hated her wig and often told her that she should show off her beautiful grey hair. She passed away in 2014, and I like the thought of her looking down on me, thinking that I did her proud. If she is, she's certainly getting her own back – what's left of my hair is now completely grey. I'll never wear a wig, though – I prefer to grow old gracefully, which I guess is what I wanted her to do.

As you might be able to tell from my scant description of my early life, I have a mental block around certain parts of my childhood. My main memories are that the island was hot most of the time, with lots of beaches, but I can't remember what I thought about living there because I was so young when I left – it was all I knew.

To say that I had a strict upbringing is an understatement, and this was largely down to my maternal grandparents. My mother's dad, whose name was George E. Roberts, was a local Methodist preacher and a sergeant at the local police station – I vaguely remember seeing him in his khaki police uniform, and I certainly felt the force of the thick black belt that he wore around his waist. I don't mean to do my grandfather an injustice, but I remember him being cold and unfeeling. My grandma was called Mary Elizabeth Roberts, but I called her 'Mammy'; everybody else called her Aunt Mem. She was a deaconess in the church and a matron at the local police station. The matriarch of the family, she ruled with an iron fist.

I think my grandparents were trying to do the best for me, and that they worried that other kids could be a bad influence. My mother was the youngest of their eight children, so they were older than my other grandparents – and she was only twenty-two when I was born, so in some ways they took on the role of parents, even before she went to England ahead of me.

Some of the other children didn't go to church, which might have been why my grandparents disapproved of their lifestyles, though I don't recall them disapproving of me being born out of wedlock. But they were always strict with me when I misbehaved. I remember one particular time I got into trouble when I was about five or six: one of my neighbours, a boy of around my age, was walking past our house. I was not allowed out to play, so he mocked me by looking up and poking out his tongue. I didn't like being teased, so I picked up a stone and threw it in his direction. I'm not sure whether I was aiming at him – I think I sort of simultaneously hoped that it both would and wouldn't hit him, if that makes sense. Anyway, the stone hit him above the right eye, and caused him to bleed profusely. He ran home in tears, and I ran into the house and hid, knowing that I was going to be in serious trouble. I wasn't able to hide for long, of course – the boy went home and told his parents what I'd done. His parents brought him round and waited to see justice being administered by my grandad, who beat me with his belt – much to the boy's satisfaction. It was a stupid thing to do – the boy could have lost an eye – and I deserved to be punished, but my body was left covered in wealds.

Another childhood beating was justified by my cheekiness. I had seen one of my aunts walking towards me. I'd normally greet her with 'Good morning, Auntie Eva', but on this particular day, I thought to myself, *I'm not going to speak to her first – let's see if she speaks to me.* She didn't say a word, and instead made a detour to my house and grassed me up, which was the signal for my grandfather to give me a hiding with his favourite belt. Auntie Eva remained present throughout my ordeal, and I remember her laughing. Never again did I make the mistake of not showing respect to my elders!

These were the days when being naughty meant a good hiding with whatever was close to hand. My grandparents would call it 'discipline', and while I would not have chosen to employ the same sort of methods if I'd had kids, I do think being encouraged to have such a strong sense of right and wrong helped me grow up to be a good person. It would also stand me in good stead in my police career.

I got used to being beaten, a word I use quite deliberately – it was much more than a mere smack. My elders believed that to teach a child how to behave, it had to hurt; they would use whatever came to hand, whether that was a belt or a wooden coat hanger. In those days, the 'moderate correction of a child by its parents or guardian' was allowed by law. While the sorts of beatings that I endured were not allowed, you would never

9

convince a West Indian in the fifties that they shouldn't punish their children. They felt it was their right.

Whips made from the branches of trees were a favourite tool of discipline, and they really left a mark. My grandfather's preferred choice was his thick leather belt, which he used to soak in urine, which somehow made it more brittle, thus elevating the pain level. The beatings would not necessarily be on my backside but could be anywhere on my body. I'm sure the NSPCC would have had kittens, but there was no such thing in the West Indies back then.

Some people still think beating children was a force for good. Despite my childhood experiences, I cannot say one way or the other – I don't think it did me any harm, but I can see how it might cause some problems in later life. I think my mother probably went along with that form of discipline because she had been punished in the same way herself – although we never spoke about it. Anyway, even if she hadn't agreed, she would never have dared to speak out against her parents – that was not the done thing at all!

I owe my grandparents a great deal – even though I often found myself on the wrong end of a beating. It was the only sort of discipline that they knew, and it worked – so why would they want to change it? When my grandma got too old to hit me, she started to punish me with ritual humiliation instead. One particular punishment that has stayed with me is being forced to wear one of her dresses. When I was naughty, she'd make me put it on before sending me to the shops to fetch something for her. She no longer needed to beat me – a fierce look and the threat of having to wear the dress would do the trick and generally kept me in line. I do not know whether having to wear a dress or getting a beating was worse, but the prospect of my schoolmates pointing and laughing at me was mortifying. Can you imagine the humiliation? Consequently, I was one of the best-behaved kids in my area. Anyway, I've never worn a dress since – not even as a joke!

As harsh as my grandmother was, I learned a lot from her – she taught me the values upon which I base my life and her strict upbringing fashioned what sort of person I was to become. It gave me a good sense of right and wrong and also helped me to endure pain and humiliation, which would prove very useful.

I was about five or six when she died. I have a vivid memory of going to her room in the middle of the night and lying on the bed next to her while she groaned in pain. One night, she was groaning more than ever – I didn't realise it at the time, but she was clearly in her last throes of death. The pain got so bad that she asked my grandad to go to the home of a female neighbour for help. As her groaning became noisier and more urgent, I remember saying, 'Don't groan so loud, Mammy.' I lay there waiting for my grandad to return, but by the time he did, she was already dead. I had no idea – I'd just done as I was told and waited until he returned.

I don't mean to do my grandfather an injustice, but I remember him being cold and unfeeling. In addition to my mother and her sister Marjorie, my grandparents had six sons – Claude, George, Jim, Leo, Frank and Basil.

Again, I know little of these siblings and remember even less. Basil had a deformity of the hand, which I can remember people referring to as a 'funny hand'. I can't remember exactly what he did, but think he was some sort of accountant. Frank, meanwhile, followed in my grandad's footsteps and became a preacher. He ended up going to live in America, along with another cousin, the Reverend Johnny Gumbs. Leo was a businessman and had a large concern in Dominica.

The other three brothers – Claude, George, and Jim – were police officers on various islands in the West Indies. I'm not sure what ranks George and Jim reached, but they must have been fairly high up because they were sent to England on secondment to be trained by the Metropolitan Police. It's strange how things turn out; they would have attended Hendon training school in the late fifties and early sixties; just a few years later, I would be the first Black British policeman to train there.

Uncle Claude – Claudius Matthias Roberts – was the eldest. He had a very successful police career, being awarded the Colonial Police Medal as well as an MBE – the story goes that he singlehandedly quelled a riot on the island of Dominica, earning the medal for his bravery. In 1972, he was instrumental in establishing the Royal Anguilla Police Force (the island was policed by officers seconded from elsewhere prior to this), and served as the island's first commissioner of police until 1977. I am told that, to this day, a portrait of him hangs in the headquarters of the Royal Anguillan Police Force in The Quarter, close to where I was born. He died in 1993 and was buried next to my grandfather, who had died twenty-five years earlier.

Next was George, followed by Jim, whose full name was James Montgomery Roberts – a very distinguished name! I prefer not to think about George – as I'll talk about later, he molested me when I was a child, having come to England to visit my mum.

I attended a nursery school in Anguilla that was next to the Ebenezer Methodist Church. When I was a little older, five or six, I attended the Valley Primary School for Boys. My most vivid memory of being there is receiving the strap from the headmaster, in front of the whole school – I'd been talking during assembly, which was against the rules. I was so shocked at being punished in this way that I wet myself, much to his glee.

I suppose I must have had some friends in Anguilla, but I can't remember much about them. It was not like growing up in the UK, where being invited to a schoolfriend's house for tea was a regular occurrence. Unless I was going to school, Sunday School or the store, I was not allowed out on my own – I would stay at home and help around the house.

The only other instance when I was allowed out was if I was

taking a message to someone. There were no buses on the island, and there were not many cars, so walking miles to school or to another district was completely normal. It was pretty safe – there was little crime, so nothing to be afraid of. Plus, everyone knew each other; if you dawdled on the way, there was always a nosey parker around to spy on you and grass you up to your parents. It was a close-knit community, and everyone seemed to be either a cousin or an uncle.

I can't think of any particularly happy memories, but nor was I unhappy – I was just a normal kid being raised by strict grand-parents. I do, however, remember one time when I sat on the steps as all my mates played, feeling so left out that I started to cry. I can look back now and say, 'I must have been lonely', but I can't remember feeling that way at the time.

September to February is hurricane season on Anguilla, which meant boarding up our windows to stop them being blown in. You knew that there had been a hurricane from the residual damage once the storm had subsided, but the tropical storms could also be very dangerous. Some of the island's houses had roofs that were made of sheets of galvanised steel, and they could be lifted right off by the wind. I once heard a story of one such sheet slicing a man clean in half. Sadly, I gather that the house I grew up in is no longer there, having been destroyed by Hurricane Irma in 2017. All that remains is the old stone oven, which sits in the middle of an empty plot.

On Sundays, we would dress in our smartest clothes and attend the Ebenezer Methodist Church. From the age of six, I was forced to attend church two or three times every Sunday – there would be a morning service, Sunday School in the after-noon and then another service in the evening. And if I ever fell asleep during a service, I would be woken up with a pinch.

I remember skipping church one day, deliberately blending in with the congregation as they left the church, and hoping I'd get away with it. Of course, I was rumbled – it hadn't occurred to me that my grandfather would be giving the sermon. He noticed that I wasn't there, and you can guess what happened – as usual, I received a good beating!

I was the youngest of all my cousins, and now I look back, I think that they might have picked on me a bit. Kids can be cruel, and I remember feeling like I was the butt of their jokes. One of the strongest memories I have of early childhood is of being on a beach surrounded by a group of taller children when one of my cousins, a teenager called Clayton Lloyd, decided to teach me to swim. He did it in a very dangerous way, dragging me out to sea, far out of my depth, and leaving me there. I was terrified and cried out for help, but everyone else thought it was hilarious. When he thought I was sufficiently far out, he swam back to the shore, leaving me to get back on my own. I can still hear him laughing as I doggy paddled – what choice did I have, if I wasn't going to drown? By the time I made it back to shore, I'd swallowed a load of saltwater. His prank could have gone horribly wrong, and I do not recommend using such cruel methods to teach someone to swim! Had I died, I don't suppose anyone would have cared too much – it would probably have been chalked down as a simple swimming accident, without any sort of investigation.

Clayton grew up to be a pilot, and I gather that when the Metropolitan Police went to Anguilla to help maintain order, he made a few bob taking the policemen to nearby islands. I later learned that he had been killed when he crashed one of his aeroplanes.

Although we never went hungry, our family was not well off, and I did not have anything near as many toys as children tend to have these days. I remember being particularly fond of a spinning top that you made whirl around by pumping a handle up and down. I had shoes, unlike some of my pals, so my family was doing better than some. However, I didn't like wearing them – I hated feeling as if I was above the people who couldn't afford them. I'd leave my shoes at home and go to school barefoot, so

I could be like the other kids. It's ironic that I took my shoes off to avoid being the odd one out in Anguilla, only to come to England and be the odd one out through no fault of my own. That's life, isn't it?

This sense of not wanting to feel superior to anyone else has continued throughout my life. Even now, I would give any of my possessions to someone else if they wanted it, even if it was something I needed myself. For example, I love collecting ties, but if someone admires the one I'm wearing, I always ask if they'd like it – and if they say yes, I'll give it to them. A couple of years ago, I was wearing a lairy shirt and someone told me that they liked it; true to form, I took it off and gave it to him, before driving home topless and feeling pleased that I'd done good. Thankfully, it was a warm day!

Christmas in Anguilla was one of my favourite times of year. Men in flamboyant costumes would go round the neighbourhood dancing on stilts, and you were expected to give them money for their efforts. Another highlight of life on the island was a fete that was held in a local park on Bank Holidays.

Since leaving Anguilla, I haven't been back once. The closest I got was in 1991, when I went on holiday to the nearby island of Antigua. Over the years I've got fed up of being asked whether Black people can get a suntan, so let me take this opportunity to clear things up. When I returned from Antigua, I lifted up my watch strap to show my colleagues that the skin underneath was significantly lighter. Having returned from the West Indies with a proper suntan, I had to take the opportunity to point it out!

This reminds me of something that people used to say to me back in the 1960s, soon after I joined the police force. I worked near Covent Garden Market, and it was a long-standing joke that whenever the market porters saw me, they would compliment me on my suntan. 'Yes,' I would always reply, 'I've been to Southend for the weekend.' I knew they were being racist – my jokey reply was the only way I knew of dealing with their idea of fun without showing them that I was hurt.

White faces were a rarity in Anguilla in my early years there; when we did see them, they tended to be American traders who had come to the island on business. Looking back, I probably stared at them in a similarly inquisitive way to the way in which I was stared at when I got to England.

I sometimes regret not going back to see where I was born, but there isn't much to take me back to the island – after all, I came to England when I was ten. Besides, it seems unlikely that anyone who still lives there would remember me – my grand-parents have long since died, and any relatives who were alive when I left would now be in their eighties at the youngest.

When I went to Antigua, the locals assumed that if you could afford to come all the way from England on holiday, you must be rich. Many people treated me as a tourist, with cab drivers in particular trying to rip me off. As soon as I opened my mouth, they could spot that I wasn't local. They clearly did not think of me as a local, but at least there was no name calling or staring. I expect they found my cockney accent strange – maybe they thought I was putting on a fancy accent to make myself sound like a white person. Nothing could be further from the truth – I was just a poor Black boy made good.

My Caribbean identity will always be important to me, but when I went back to the West Indies in 1991, I felt like a fish out of water. It has always seemed strange to me, but while I received good wishes from people all over the world during the course of my career in the police force, I cannot ever remember receiving any congratulations from the West Indies, nor from my home island. It added to the feeling that I'd severed my connections with the country of my birth. I occasionally found myself wondering whether people there were jealous that I'd made it to England and been successful; perhaps they just didn't care, a thought that I found difficult to confront – I've always been proud to come from Anguilla.

2

The Only Black Boy in Bromley

IN 1956, I BOARDED the *Napoli* and sailed across the Atlantic Ocean to England. The ship, which was operated by Flotta Lauro Lines, would be converted to a freight liner four years later, before being scrapped in 1971.

Being only ten years old, I've no idea how long I was at sea, but it must have been several weeks. In fact, I can't remember much about the journey at all. I think I slept in a bunk bed, and I know that I was looked after by an uncle or cousin who was emigrating to England at the same time – though we lost touch with them soon after we arrived. I didn't stay in touch with anyone back in Anguilla after I left. I was just a little boy, after all.

We sailed to Calais and on to Southampton, before taking the train to London Victoria. It is a wonder that I didn't get lost in the huge crowds of people that were making the journey. I seem to remember being smartly dressed, in long trousers, a jacket and tie, together with a pork-pie hat – I'd been told that it would be so cold in England that if I didn't wear a hat, I would get a head cold and would probably die. It was so cold there, I was led to believe, that in the winter the snow would be as high as mountains. That was all I knew about England. I don't think anyone in Anguilla knew anything about England, because none of them had been there, and I certainly hadn't heard any suggestion that people there would be racist. I've no idea what my life would have been like if I hadn't left, but I'm very glad that I did.

I was travelling on my own because I was following my mother, who had made the journey with her sister Marjorie a few years before, leaving me to be looked after by my grand-parents. She had sailed on the *Antilles* from Guadeloupe to Plymouth, arriving on 17 September 1954. The immigration records indicate that prior to crossing the Atlantic she was resi-dent in St Kitts, which is a bit of a mystery to me; it might have been that she moved there from Anguilla in order to earn money to pay for the fare. I cannot say for sure what made her decide to leave the West Indies, but I guess she'd been told that there was lots of money to be made abroad. Like many other people who came from the Caribbean as part of the Windrush gener-ation, they were told that the need for workers on the other side of the Atlantic was so great that they would find a job easily.

My mum did not send me any pictures of England. I expect she wrote me letters to tell me what life was like, but I was so young at the time that I can't remember. I can remember her telling me that I would join her at some point – and I know that once she arrived, she worked four jobs in order to save up for the fare that would bring me to England, starting work at four o'clock in the morning. It was common to have multiple jobs at a time when they were each so poorly paid.

My Aunt Marjorie went on to train as a nurse and would later emigrate to America. My mum had also wanted to be a nurse, but she ended up as a companion to a wealthy elderly lady, having seen the job advertised in a magazine that was distributed by the Methodist Church. The lady lived in Bromley in Kent, an area that would provide my first view of England.

There's a subtle difference between a servant and a compan-ion; the fact that my mother was the latter implies that she was treated as something of an equal. She lived in the same house as her mistress, in adjoining rooms – a far cry from servant's quar-ters! That lady, whose name was Edith Le Pers, treated my mother very well and I'm still grateful to her for accepting us without question. Miss Le Pers was a lovely woman; even though my mum was employed to look after her house, we were more like family. In those days, having Black people in your house would have been unpopular with large sections of the population; Miss Le Pers's next-door neighbours refused to talk to her when she allowed us to stay with her. But she was prepared to put up with criticism in order to do what she thought was right – she really stuck her neck out. I've often wondered if she got any nasty letters – you know the type, the ones sent anonymously that might have said she was a 'nigger lover'. I know for a fact that she lost some of her friends – she even had relatives who never spoke to her again – but she didn't care. The most important thing to her was her Christian faith, and she did everything she could to treat my mum and me well. One of my greatest regrets is that I didn't ever have the chance to properly show my appreciation and thank her for making us feel so welcome in her home.

I can still vividly remember the feeling of walking down the steps at Victoria Station and being surrounded by white faces, having been met by my mother and Miss Le Pers. We travelled by train to Bromley. I'd never seen a train before that – not even a picture of one – so I must have felt like a kid let loose in a sweet shop. What a transformation from my life in the West Indies!

Miss Le Pers, who had never married, lived in a large semi-detached house with a big garden in an affluent part of Bromley, a town popular with people who commuted to work in the City – the 'stockbroker belt'. The luxuries in her house were a long way from what I was used to. Back in Anguilla, there was no proper plumbing; all we had was an outside toilet and a shower room off the kitchen, both of which used water from the cistern in the yard that collected rainwater from the roof. As you can imagine, I was fascinated by the fact that I could switch on lights and had hot and cold running water 'on tap' – little things that were generally taken for granted in England.

We never called Miss Le Pers by her first name, and it occurs to me now that we'd always call our elders by their surnames. Funnily enough, this habit remains with me even now – I prefer to call elders by their surnames, prefaced by Mr, Mrs or Miss, and find it uncomfortable when I'm asked to use their Christian name. To my mind, it's a way of showing respect.

Miss Le Pers had a car, which in those days was still something of a luxury – especially for me, given that I'd never travelled in one before. It was an Austin, and I can still remember the registration mark: FKM 140. Miss Le Pers was an overly cautious and nervous driver, but thankfully there was not much traffic on the roads in those days, so accidents were easily avoided. She had a sister who lived in a mental institution in Dartford – she'd drive us there on Sundays and we'd wait in the car while she went in to see her. I think she may also have had other relatives in Bellingham or Catford, but they didn't speak to her because of us.

You must remember that I was only ten years old at this point, and far from worldly-wise. I can still remember watching television for the first time. It was black and white, and the service finished at midnight; following the national anthem, a white spot would appear in the middle of the screen and a piercing sound would remind the viewer to turn off the set. It was at around this time that I used a telephone for the first time, too.

I've already alluded to the negative response that greeted our presence in the neighbourhood. Although people had been coming to Britain from the Caribbean to help fill post-war labour shortages for nearly a decade by this point – the ship HMT *Empire Windrush*, after which the 'Windrush Generation' were christened, docked in Tilbury on 22 June 1948 – there were not many Black people in Bromley, and there were certainly none on our street. And of course, our next-door neighbours did not speak to me or my mum, which made us feel unwelcome – a bit like second-class citizens. Once, when we planted some flowers in Miss Le Pers's front garden, some of them were even pulled up by not-so-nice neighbours, who killed the others with weedkiller. They must have seen us planting them and decided that we didn't deserve the pleasure of watching them flourish; the only thing to be grateful for was that we did not have to suffer physical violence.

As a Black person in those days, it was difficult to buy property. In fact, if you wanted to simply rent a room, signs in the windows of boarding houses that said 'No blacks, no Irish, no dogs' and 'No niggers' would make it very clear that you weren't welcome. I'd be lying if I said that such racist attitudes didn't affect us – of course they did – but we saw it as being just the way things were. We would simply walk past those signs, though we might quicken our pace slightly or cross the road and pretend that we hadn't noticed them.

The fact that Miss Le Pers was able to ignore the prejudice that existed around Black people shows that she must have been very strong. As far as I can remember, she was never provoked into a row with her judgemental, small-minded neighbours. She must have been a special kind of person and a true Christian.

Eventually, one of the neighbours, a bloke called Lesley Cullen, started talking to us at the church that we all went to. He was a commissioner of oaths – a fact that he advertised with a sign outside his house – and he would later play a big part in my life when he changed my surname by deed poll in 1968. He didn't charge me for the work, which showed how far he'd come from the days when he'd completely ignored us – when we first moved to Bromley, it had been as if we didn't exist. I was well known by this time, and I suppose he was beginning to realise that we did not present a threat to him or his family after all.

Despite Mr Cullen's friendliness, other neighbours continued to make the usual distasteful remarks. Miss Le Pers had some racist next-door neighbours with a daughter of about my age. She would always smile at me, being careful not to do so when her parents were around. In fact, if we were in our garden when she was in hers, her parents would call her indoors. They were so small-minded that they would even take their dog inside with them – after one particular occasion when they spotted it coming up to the fence and wagging its tail at us.

I've no idea how they would have reacted if they'd known that I often spoke to their daughter; our respective schools organised ballroom dance classes that were held at the local girls' school and run by the Peggy Spencer School of Dancing. We both attended, and we even danced together on a number of occasions. However, when I saw her in her back garden, she would completely ignore me – she was clearly keen not to incur the wrath of her parents. We were just innocent schoolkids, but her parents would have disowned her had they known that she actually spoke to me – let alone danced with me!

Life in England took some getting used to. Can you imagine how I felt when I saw snow or fog for the first time? Such things were completely wondrous to me – a little boy who was used to a very different life.

It was at St Mark's Primary School in Bromley that I made my first white friend. Wallace Cole and I became blood brothers, copying something that we'd seen done in a film between a white cowboy and a Native American when we went to the pictures together one Saturday morning. We each cut our hand and joined the blood in the cuts – it felt like the right thing to do, as we were best friends. Wallace, his brother Barry and their parents treated me like one of their own and made me feel very welcome. If Wallace was given tuppence to buy sweets from the shops, his mum always made sure that I had tuppence, too.

Wallace and Barry's parents, whose names were Ciss and Wally, used to invite me and my mum to their prefab every weekend for afternoon tea. Just like Miss Le Pers, they were brave to do this, knowing that showing solidarity and kindness to their Black acquaintances was unlikely to be accepted by the community. Wally was a bus driver, based at Bromley Bus Garage. He and his wife found themselves being ostracised by their neighbours, suffering abuse and ridicule for befriending a Black person, but they chose to lose the friendship of their neighbours rather than to join the rest of the community in subjecting us to a less-than-friendly welcome. I can still remember Mrs Cole standing up for me when I was being bullied at school because of the colour of my skin. She was not afraid to stand up for herself, and she did exactly the same for me. All this was happening at a time when if you were white and befriended a Black person, you would be abused with racial slurs; as a result, such friendships were a rarity. The Cole family very good friends to us. They later emigrated to Australia, and my mum would show our gratitude to them by sending them parcels of treats.

3

Growing Up

I WAS, OF COURSE, the only Black boy in my class at primary school. I didn't realise it at the time, but this was just the first in a long line of occasions throughout my life when I would be 'the first'. However, at school, the racial barriers that were so problematic elsewhere didn't seem to exist; I would play with all the other children, joining in with games like hopscotch and tag. I also learned to play football and rounders. I was good at cricket, as this was the game I'd played in the West Indies.

I have no memories of being stared at by the other children, but I can remember that my classmates were endlessly amused by my hair – its texture was different from what they were used to. It was black and curly in those days, and they would always ask me if they could touch it. The first time I let them, they were shocked and exclaimed that it felt like touching a wire brush, much to my embarrassment. If I'd been more enterprising, I would have charged everyone who wanted to touch it a penny – I'd have made a fortune. I can also remember everyone at school wanting to know why the palms of my hands and the soles of my feet were white when my skin was brown. I didn't know the answer but was keen to be liked, so I said that I would try to find out.

After a while, I got used to being stared at, reminding myself that lots of people in Bromley had never seen a Black person before, let alone touched one. Televisions were still pretty rare at that point, too, which only added to the problem and made me feel like even more of a rarity. I had to get used to being called names as I walked down the street. I sometimes noticed that people would cross over to the other side of the road to avoid me when I was walking towards them. Sometimes it almost felt like they were frightened of me.

'Black Sambo' was a derogatory term that had been used ever since the nineteenth century, becoming especially popular in America during the era of racial segregation. The name also appeared in the title of a late-nineteenth-century children's book, *The Story of Little Black Sambo*, written by the Scottish author Helen Bannerman in 1899. It was not intended to be offensive – indeed, the Black characters were portrayed positively, with one of them being the hero of the story. However, by the time I was at school in the 1950s, the name had become a racial slur.

Black Sambo was also the name of a brand of bubble gum – long since taken off the market – that was black, and the packet featured a picture of a little Black boy with exaggerated thick lips blowing a bubble. Another sweet that was popular in those days was Black Jacks. I thought 'Black Jack' had quite a nice ring to it; I remember joking with my classmates that I should consider changing my name to Jack! Looking back on my childhood, it seems that I had little choice but to accept that this was what it was like to live in a country where I was in the minority; I just learned to shrug my shoulders, but it wasn't always easy.

I was very respectful towards my teachers. After all, it came naturally to me – this was how I'd been brought up. But I struggled to understand the actions of the headmistress, who refused to let me attend grammar school. It happened after I'd taken the eleven-plus; I passed the exam, only for her to say to my mother, 'Although Norwell has passed the eleven-plus, we cannot send him to a grammar school – he has to learn the English ways.' I cannot say for certain what she meant, but I can have a pretty good guess – it seems like she was doing everything she could to avoid sending a clever Black boy to a grammar school. It seems clear to me that her actions were racially motivated. She thought that sending a Black boy to a grammar school ahead of a white boy would lead to criticism from white parents whose children did not make it.

Being denied a place at grammar school could have seriously affected my future, but it turned out not to really matter – it just made me more determined to succeed off my own back. I now think of what happened as my first real exposure to institutional racism. My mother chose not to kick up a fuss – as with other types of discrimination that we suffered, we simply accepted that those were the rules – though that did not stop me from feeling like I'd been cheated.

Despite the racial prejudice that I found myself facing, life as a young boy in Bromley could be fun. I enjoyed Saturday-morning trips to the pictures at the Gaumont, a cinema on the high street. I would go with my friends Wallace and Barry; it would cost sixpence to get in and we'd watch Westerns, cheering when the goodies inevitably triumphed.

As happy as life sometimes was, I had few close friends apart from Wallace, Barry and another boy from my class called Mark Churchill. I joined the Boy Scouts and the Boys' Brigade, and can remember going to the meetings, taking part and then coming straight home – I don't remember going on any of the camps or excursions those groups are so renowned for. And I obviously didn't have any Black friends – after all, there were barely any other Black people in Bromley!

Where I lived, there were plenty of parks to play in. There were also fields just up the road from where we lived, but these have long since been built on. We would think nothing of getting on our bikes and going to the woods. In fact, we once left Bromley early one morning and cycled all the way to

Hastings, about fifty miles away, just to eat our sandwiches on the beach before cycling back by mid-afternoon.

In those days, cycling was my passion. From a young age in Bromley, I learned how to take a bike to bits, clean the parts and reassemble it. In fact, this fondness for bike maintenance was nearly my undoing; while racing one of my mates, and about to overtake him, something went wrong and I flew over the handlebars. The next thing I knew, I was in hospital suffering from concussion. If I appear a bit stupid nowadays, I can always put it down to the blow on my head – that's my excuse and I'm sticking to it!

I had another skirmish that landed me in hospital. While play-fighting with sticks with my friend Mark and another lad, one of them broke and a splinter became imbedded in my left eye. A doctor pulled it out with tweezers, while I was wide awake – it bloody well hurt, I can tell you. The same eye was struck with a squash racquet many years later, when my partner played a shot and accidentally followed through with his racket. The pain was excruciating and I fell to the ground, temporarily blinded. There was blood all over the squash court, and I was in St Thomas's Hospital for a week while my sight recovered.

When I was a child, my mother and I went to the Methodist church in Bromley every Sunday, until one week something happened that left us feeling unwelcome. The service had just finished, and the minister was standing by the church door, shaking hands with the parishioners as they left. When my mother and I got to the front of the queue and were waiting to be greeted, he seemed to deliberately avoid doing so, instead moving past us and shaking hands with the person behind us in the queue. We didn't understand what had happened and felt very insulted, but we didn't make a fuss – being discriminated against was par for the course in those days.

I'll leave it to you to consider why else a man of the cloth, who was supposed to teach love and tolerance, would treat us, his only Black parishioners, with such disdain. However, although his actions were, at least to my twelve-year-old mind, a long way from what I regarded as Christian behaviour, they had no bearing on my religious belief. I'd been raised as a Christian and was taught to be generous and kind to others. In the face of discrimination, there was just one aspect of Christian belief that I struggled with: the suggestion that I should be able to turn the other cheek. I'm still a Christian, but I don't go to church any more. And I must confess that if someone smacked me on the left cheek, they should expect to be smacked twice as hard in response – and on both cheeks! Being able to stand up for yourself is important. I suppose my difficulty in turning the other cheek comes from having to put up with so much. I've suffered enough injustice that I can recognise it, and it makes me want to help others. Having said that, there are many different ways of responding, and physically fighting back is just one of them. Violence should only ever be a last resort; I think of myself as a 'mental fighter', and my mental strength has saved me on many occasions.

After this unfortunate incident at church, my mother and I started to go to the local Baptist church, where we were made to feel more welcome. Miss Le Pers was also ostracised by the Methodist church because of her association with us; fortunately she was able to put up with it. When the headmistress of my primary school said that I had to 'learn the English ways', was this cruelty one of the 'ways' to which she was referring?

Until we left the Methodist Church, I was also a member of the youth club that was attached to it, which meant playing various games as well as activities like judo and dancing. It was through the youth club that I met Graham and Wendy Clarke, a 'beatnik' couple who would have a major impact on my life. Graham had a bushy beard and they both dressed in a style that would have been described as 'way out'. They are one of the only couples I know who have been together since their teens

– they are still going strong, some sixty-five years later! They were just a few years older than me, but I soon looked up to Graham as a hero, because as well as being a jolly nice person, he could dance and jive, play the piano, the violin and an assortment of musical instruments. By contrast, I was happy playing the kazoo!

Graham had the idea of forming a band and asked me to be involved. We were called 'The Ebenezer Three'; the other member of the group was a bloke I called Digby Rigby. I played double bass, but I didn't know how to play it at all – I'd hang it around my neck as if it were a guitar. We played at Methodist Association youth clubs all over the country, culminating in a concert at the Royal Albert Hall, and we ended up being quite a hit. I can still remember one of the songs we played, a number called 'Joshua Fought the Battle of Jericho'. I sang in a West Indian dialect, rolling my eyes as I did, which went down a treat with the audience. We'd regularly be asked for an encore.

I'm still friends with Graham, more than sixty years after we first met. An artist of some renown, he has a studio in Maidstone, and he and Wendy have adopted me as one of their family. I've often found myself wishing they were my real parents – they were much more caring than my real mum and dad; I can't ever remember my mum putting her arms around me and giving me a hug. I don't know why Graham and Wendy took me, a poor little Black boy, under their wing, but I'm very glad that they did. I call them Mum and Dad, and I go to see them every Christmas morning. They have three children of their own – Abigail, Jason and Emily – who I've known pretty much their whole lives. I call Abigail 'sis' and she calls me 'bro'.

4

Secondary School

WITH THE LOCAL grammar school not an option that was open to me, I went to the local secondary modern, smartly dressed in a shiny new school uniform. Again, I was the only Black boy in the school, which felt even more daunting at a bigger school, and I soon became a target for abuse. I hadn't been there very long before those aforementioned fifth formers dropped me on my head to see the colour of my blood. One of them, despite being sixteen years old, was already the size of a fully grown man. I was taken to hospital and had two stitches; I still have a scar on my forehead, more than six decades later. I have no idea what they expected to find, but I can only imagine the look on their faces when they saw that my blood was the same as theirs!

What happened next was a sharp and painful life lesson. When my mother and Wallace Cole's mother went to the school to complain, the headmaster fobbed them off, dismissing the actions of my attackers as nothing more than 'boys being boys'. I'll leave it to you to decide whether the matter was taken sufficiently seriously. When they didn't receive any sort of apology, I'm quite sure that Mrs Cole would have given the headmaster a gobful. I cannot help but wonder what would happen to the bullies if they did the same thing today – though I'd like to think that such racist bullying is a thing of the past. We were powerless to complain, and that was just what it was like to be the only Black family in the community. I can't explain how it felt, but I wish I could take people back there and show them.

Such brutality was nothing new to me given the frequency with which I'd been beaten throughout my childhood, and corporal punishment remained a popular method of discipline at secondary school. I remember getting the slipper from the French teacher for the simple reason that I was not able to master his subject – sometimes the playing field felt so far from level that I had to be at least twice as good as my peers to get the same treatment. I also got the cane from the headmaster for talking in class. If you were quick about it, you could take the opportunity to stuff a couple of exercise books down your trousers to soften the blows; however, the teachers soon got wind of that and started to administer the cane on our hands when giving you what they called 'six of the best'.

Some people think kids would be better behaved if corporal punishment still existed in schools, and as old-fashioned as it might seem, I can see their point. But I also remember the teachers who began to take delight in administering the punishment, with relish and a glint in their eyes.

Though I was the only Black boy, an Asian boy called Geoffrey Dubois joined the school in 1958, when I was twelve, and he was made fun of in a similar way to me. Some of the boys cruelly called him 'Piss Tank', as they said he always smelled of urine. I don't know why, but the bullying he was suffering didn't cause me to identify with him. I knew not to call him Piss Tank, but I didn't stop other people from doing it – whereas now, I absolutely would.

It was clear that I was among the poorest children at the school, which made me stand out even more; some of my classmates seemed incomparably wealthy, and I can remember them coming into school having been on foreign holidays to

Switzerland and France. My mum could not afford to take me to such places, but it didn't bother me. I never went on holiday, but we did occasionally go to the seaside. I remember going on the steam train and sticking our heads out of the windows as we were racing along, not realising that what we were doing was incredibly dangerous. It was funny – Wallace's face was as black as mine from the soot that blew into our faces!

Wallace and Barry Cole both received free school meals, and their mother arranged for me to have them, too. It was very kind of her, but I hated getting them – there was an unpleasant stigma attached to having to queue up separately, with everyone knowing that you were poor. Very often, I would choose to go without any lunch – going hungry was preferable to being looked down on.

My mother always had a lot of housework to do for Miss Le Pers, and it would go without saying that I had to help out before and after school. I would cut the lawn using a push mower, as well as doing some of the shopping and helping with cleaning. I didn't mind doing such chores – I'd been brought up to enjoy housework, although I hesistated at hanging Miss Le Pers's big old-fashioned bloomers on the clothes line – they looked so long that they would have stretched all the way to her knees. Another thing that I remember about Miss Le Pers is that she had white straggly hair, which she would regularly go to have styled at a hairdresser. She also had a fair bit of facial hair, which I'd never seen on a woman before.

It was partly because money was so tight that I had been brought up to look after my clothes. If my shoes became worn out because I'd been playing football in the playground, that was my problem – like it or not, they would have to last me the whole term, if not the whole year. When they had holes in them, my mother wouldn't be able to afford a new pair – instead, the old ones would be resoled and reheeled. Similarly, socks were darned and clothes were repaired – we had no choice but to 'make do and mend'. I would have been happy to go to a charity shop – some of the clothes that I've donated to charity since then were better than some of the stuff I had to wear during my schooldays – but there weren't as many charity shops around in those days.

5

'Persistent Mental Cruelty'

WHILE WE WERE living in Bromley, my mother married a man who would become my stepfather, but it was a union that was doomed to fail. I've no idea how they met – all I know is that when my mum met him, one of her brothers announced that he came from a place in Dominica called Boetica. One of my other uncles warned my mum, 'Be careful – nothing good can come out of Boetica.' He was implying that people from this region tended to be dodgy geezers, which did indeed turn out to be the case.

Although she had been warned about her new husband, my mum didn't pay any attention – she was in love and she was happy, at least until the abuse started. Her new husband was a vicious, sadistic man who took delight in making her suffer. While he was regularly physically abusive to me, he never knocked her about; instead, he wore her down mentally, which was just as harmful. I guess these days we'd call his treatment of her 'gaslighting' – he undermined her, chipping away at her self-confidence. Much later, when she was eventually granted a divorce, he would be found guilty of 'persistent mental cruelty'. My mum ended up getting dementia in her old age, but I think the unhappiness of her marriage had a long-term effect – it made her nervous, and she was never the same again.

My mother's husband really was a nasty piece of work; it was all that I could do to keep my hands off him, but if I'd dared to take such action in my mother's defence, I think my career path would have been somewhat different! And, of course, there was fear – this was a man who once bit one of my fingers right to the bone.

After my mother married this man, in 1960, we moved out of Miss Le Pers's house – my new stepfather worked on the railways and was based at Camden Town, so we moved to North London to join him. Our new home was a one-bedroom flat on Edis Street, not far from Regent's Park. It was far from an ideal arrangement – I'd often have to sleep on the floor in the same room that my mother and her husband slept in. The sort of accommodation that we lived in was referred to as 'living in rooms'; we didn't have our own toilet and bathroom, instead having to share these facilities with the other people who lived in the flat.

Nowadays, such an arrangement would be regarded as unhealthy, but it was common in an overpopulated city with limited housing. In one of the places where we lived, there was no bath; in order to wash, I'd have to go to the public baths once a week. This was especially welcome in the winter. You'd put a shilling in a meter, which would cause a bath to be filled with exactly the right amount of hot water. They had it calibrated down to a fine art – just enough hot water was delivered before the taps started running cold.

It was at around this time that I was indecently assaulted by my mum's brother George, which was one of the worst experiences of my entire life. It happened when he came to England for a holiday and was staying with us in London. Our flat was so small that we were all sleeping in the same room – my mum and stepfather were at one end of the bed and I was at the other with George. I remember what happened like it was yesterday – I was just lying there, frozen with fear as I felt him rubbing himself up against me. I knew what he was doing and I knew it was wrong, but I said nothing. The next day, he gave me two shillings and sixpence, which I suppose was to keep me quiet. It seems like a tiny amount now, but in those days it was a lot of money to a young boy.

I think now that George had been grooming me beforehand, but I can't remember how – I've blocked everything out. I didn't tell anyone about it and nor did I confront him about his behaviour – I knew that I would never be believed if I reported him. Think about it – this was someone who was outwardly respectable, a police officer and a pillar of society back home in the West Indies. Plus, he was married with children himself, which makes what he did even more shocking. How could I possibly tell my mother that her own brother was a paedophile? Apart from the fact that she wouldn't have believed me, she'd have kicked me from pillar to post – as her reaction when I finally told her some four decades later showed. She tore me off a strip and became defensive, before accusing me of making the whole thing up. Had I told her when the abuse was actually happening, I would have received a severe beating, at the very least. I suppose that this is why so many paedophiles get away with child abuse and many victims are too scared to tell anyone. I often find myself wondering if George did the same thing to any other children. I can't even get angry about it any more, but I hope that talking about what I went through will help people who have suffered similar abuse and might be too frightened to talk about it. I never heard anything about him after that, but I do know that he's dead now.

Shortly after this incident, we moved again, to a house on Jamestown Road in Camden Town, where I had my own room. During these dark days in my childhood, I attended Haverstock Comprehensive School in Chalk Farm. Money was still tight, of course, so I did a paper round before school each morning, as well as a milk round on Saturdays – I had to earn my keep, and I was expected to contribute to the household funds. I also managed to get a job working at a vegetarian restaurant in Earls Court, doing the washing up and cleaning the floors. I was paid thirty shillings a week, which was a decent wage. The owner of the restaurant was a guy called Alan Palmer, who was a good boss and trusted me completely. He used to go home at the end of a night, leaving me alone to finish scrubbing the floors; he'd tell me to take thirty shillings for my wages plus my fare home and then to lock up the restaurant, posting the keys through the front door. I never ripped him off and took exactly what he told me to; it was at this point that I learned a maxim that has been important to me ever since: 'A man who is trusted will always trust himself.' Being trusted by my boss made me feel grown-up and responsible. One other benefit of working there was that I could eat as much food as I wanted – as much as I enjoyed it, it did not turn me into a vegetarian!

The first thing I noticed at my new school was that there were lots of Black and brown students and no one really stared at me. I was soon quite popular and had a bit of a gang – there were six of us and we would go round together. We all dressed the same way, copied one another's mannerisms and even walked the same – looking back at it now, we must have seemed like a poor man's version of the Sharks or the Jets from *West Side Story*!

We weren't a gang in the modern sense of the word – we didn't go round beating anyone up or knifing anyone – it was just an old-fashioned, wholesome friendship. My friends in the group were Derek Johnson, Ernie Toop, Neil Birchenough, Alex Watts and Ernie Neighbour, and we spent all our free time together. I often went to their houses for tea, but they were never allowed to come to mine – my stepfather would never permit that, and my mum had no choice but to side with him.

I introduced my pals to the youth club that I attended in Muswell Hill, which was affiliated to the Methodist Association of Youth Clubs. We would meet up and take a bus from Camden Town to Muswell Hill each Friday night, and when we got there we would listen to music, dance and sit around eating sandwiches, before getting the bus back home at around 10 or 11 p.m. Up-and-coming local bands would play at the club – one of them was a local band called The Kinks, who you might just have heard of! The only thing that I was never able to persuade my 'gang' to do was accompany me to church.

I still exchange Christmas cards with Ernie Neighbour and was friendly with Neil Birchenough until his death in 2021. I also made a point of visiting their mums while they were still alive – they'd been good to me at a time in my life when I needed friends, and I wanted to show my gratitude. After I joined the police, I went to see Neil's mum in Camden Town with some meat from the butchers; I also visited Ernie's mum when I was working at Albany Street Police Station because she lived nearby. I felt honoured when I was invited to her funeral.

Someone else I'm still I touch with from those days is the wife of the youth club leader, who is now in her eighties. Even now, I ring her once a week, and a few years ago I went to visit her in Torquay. She and her husband were kind to us lads, and I'm always keen to repay such kindnesses if I'm able. In fact, she has asked me to give the eulogy at her funeral; if I'm still around, it will be my pleasure to fulfil this promise.

I only ever got into one fight during my school days. It happened outside the school gates, and I seem to recall that it was over a girl. I was minding my own business when a huge sixth former – he must have been over six feet tall – came up to me and said that he'd seen me talking to a girl he fancied. After he'd warned me off her, he took a swing at me, only for me to duck and push him over. He fell over and cut his ear on the pavement; in the commotion, a crowd gathered to watch and began to cheer. His ear was bleeding profusely, and his shirt was soon covered with blood. When a teacher noticed what was going on, we all scarpered.

I'm not proud of it now, but standing up for myself in this way gained me respect, and I had an easier time after that. One other thing that helped was that I was made a prefect, a role that came with certain privileges, including being able to stay inside during breaktime – particularly welcome in the winter.

As a boy from a poor background, my mum could not afford to buy me trendy clothes, so I was glad that a school uniform was compulsory – it helped me fit in with my peers. I was also pleased that both the area and the school were thoroughly multi-racial. The indignity of having to suffer racial slurs, as I had in Bromley, was generally in the past, though I remember walking home from seeing a mate of mine one time and passing four 'hard nuts' – what we called young thugs in those days – sitting on a wall. I could have crossed over the road and walked on the other side of the street, but this time I decided not to. When one of them shouted 'Hey, Sambo!', I turned around and walked back to them. I'd been putting up with this for ages and was fed up of it. 'Who's the man with the big mouth?' I said, 'I'll take him on now.' I didn't know what I was saying – I was in dream-land. They could have done anything, but I was lucky that they backed down. As I walked off, I said, 'I'll see any of you again when you're on your own.' I think they were shocked that I'd dared to face up to them. I did not wait for them to change their minds and walked away feeling like a million dollars – I'd made my mark. Of course, I was also lucky – if things had gone the other way, I could have got badly beaten up.

Looking back on it now, I'm glad that I stood up for myself; I'd had every insult thrown at me when I was in Bromley, and I had no intention of putting up with it again. I had to make a stand, and this seemed like the right time. The difference in Camden was that I was no longer the only one – I was at a school where there were plenty of other Black and Asian kids, and no one called me names there. It was an improving picture. My threat wasn't an idle one – I would definitely have fought the bloke who'd had such a big mouth in front of his mates. From experience, such men usually turn out to be cowards when someone stands up to them.

Despite the fact that I now lived in an area of London that was a lot more racially diverse, I still had no Black friends. I don't know why this was – perhaps it was a result of being brought up in a uniformly white community in suburban Bromley; I often wondered whether my outlook on life would have been different if I'd grown up somewhere like Brixton. I guess that if I had lived there, I may have never lost my West Indian accent.

I don't remember ever receiving the cane at my London secondary school; the teachers there didn't thrash their students when they didn't understand something, a very different approach from my school in Bromley. The plain fact is that some people – and I include myself in this category – are not as academically minded as others. There were some subjects that came to me pretty easily, but in others I found that if you didn't keep up with the lessons you would get left behind, as the teachers just did not have time to treat you as an individual. Of course, some teachers were better than others. They all knew what they were talking about, but some of them seemed to be unable – or unwilling – to explain it to the students. It could also have been that I was just too thick to understand what they were talking about!

For instance, I remember struggling to stop myself laughing when the physics teacher was giving a lesson about magnetism and mentioned a two-foot-long magnet – to me, it just seemed like a really ridiculous idea. He asked me what was so funny, ridiculing me in front of the whole class to the extent that I wished I could dig a big hole under the desk and jump into it. 'Don't show your ignorance, boy,' he said. 'You can get magnets two *miles* long.' I still didn't have a clue what he was talking about, but I thought better than to ask him for a further explanation. My mates who were good at physics must have thought I was stupid. When I think about my schooldays now, I wish that I'd studied more and attained better qualifications, but it's easy to be wise after the event.

Not long before I was due to take my O Levels, I was ill with chicken pox, tonsillitis and pneumonia, and one of my mates from school came to visit me and bring me some homework. There was no chair in my bedroom, so I took one from the landing of our flat into my room for my friend to sit on. My stepfather thought this was unreasonable behaviour, and when my guest had left, he beat me savagely – he really was a complete bully. But it was fortunate that I didn't retaliate; a criminal record would have scuppered my chances of joining the police.

I left school at the age of sixteen, with just two O Levels – in religious education and chemistry. I had failed English, biology, geography, physics and maths, which I put down to my illness just before the exams. I was, however, happy with the two I passed – my marks in each of these subjects were so high that I was awarded a prize. Up to this point, I had wanted to be a doctor, but it was clear to me once my exam results came through that I was not clever enough for that. I then wanted to be a physical training instructor, but this would be impossible too – it required English and maths.

It wasn't just the illness that had disrupted my last year at school – when I was still fifteen, my stepfather had kicked me out. It happened soon after the incident I mentioned before, when I moved the chair to my bedroom for my friend to sit on; after he knocked me about a bit, he threw me out of the house. I remember being dismayed that my mum didn't stick up for me, but I'm now able to understand that she was probably too afraid of him – after all, he was abusive to her, too. I left with the clothes I was wearing and nothing else.

I had nowhere to go and was completely desperate. If things had been different, I could have ended up living on the streets, but I was lucky that my destiny was to take me on a different path. I went to see Alan Palmer, the owner of the restaurant where I worked, and told him what had happened. I was fifteen at this point – I didn't realise that, being a minor, I couldn't just leave home and shack up with anyone who would have me. Alan allowed me to stay at his place for the night, before contacting the children's department at the local council the next day. I ended up staying at a school summer camp, where I was given clothes and food. I've often wondered whether Alan paid for my stay.

At this point, my three half-siblings – one boy and two girls – hadn't been born. They came along after I'd been kicked out, and I didn't grow up with them. They were brought up in England, and it always seemed that, compared to me, they were able to get away with murder – perhaps that was a difference between being brought up in the West Indies and in England. They also idolised their dad, but that's another story. I'd later move back in with my mum and stepdad, but only briefly – my stepfather's verbal and physical abuse meant that any reunion was doomed to failure. It was around this time, when I attempted to stick up for her, that he bit my finger, leaving a wound that required two stitches.

When my mum finally plucked up the courage to leave my stepfather, the situation culminated in a messy divorce. He was accused of persistent mental cruelty at Clerkenwell Magistrates' Court; I was called as a witness and spoke in defence of my mother. My stepfather denied the allegations, but was found guilty due to our evidence. The sentence he received was pathetic; he pleaded poverty and got a couple of 'moody' payslips that made it look like he was earning less than he really was. He had to pay ten shillings for her and just five shillings for each of the three children he and my mother had together – a pittance.

After my mother's divorce, she and her three children ended up living back in Bromley with Miss Le Pers, effectively acting as her carer until she died on 28 December 1970. She left my mum her house in her will, as well as ten or twelve other properties that she'd rented out during her life. I'd never known her to have a job, but she'd go round to all these houses, collecting rent. In those days, they were only worth a couple of grand each. If my mum had handled the situation properly, she could have been financially comfortable, but she ended up using a solicitor who ripped her off. She got a few bob, but nothing compared to what she'd have got if she'd kept them and rented them out.

My mum wasn't happy living in New Farm Avenue without Miss Le Pers, so she moved to Catford. I wanted her to come and live with me in North London – at one point, the house next door was being sold and I wanted to buy it for her – but she chose to be close to my half-brother and sisters. She lived down there for the rest of her life, and our relationship became a bit strained. Although we grew apart, she was never far from my thoughts.

6

Westfield College

AFTER I'D LEFT school, I needed to find a full-time job, and one of my first interviews was for a job as a scientific laboratory technician for Westfield College in Hampstead, part of the University of London. I got the job and started work in the botany department.

Laboratory technicians play an important role in a university's science department; it was my responsibility to prepare and test experiments for the students. Sometimes I had to make bits of apparatus, an aspect of the work that I found particularly rewarding. I dare say that there are renowned doctors, professors and scientists whose careers I played a small but important role in fashioning. I enjoyed the work a great deal, although I was less keen on the field trips – I have vivid memories of being up to my waist in mud while collecting specimens of moss from a peat bog!

I was just sixteen when I started at Westfield, and it was my first proper job. Some of the professors and doctors that I worked alongside were from overseas and had come to London to conduct research. It was a very ethnically diverse workplace – as well as the staff, the students came from all over the world to study there – but there was no hint of racism. I was accepted on my merits; everyone realised that I had a job to do and was keen to learn.

I'll let you in on a slightly embarrassing secret. It was while I was working at the college that I learned about the importance of using deodorant. My boss, a lovely man called John Burns, told me, quite frankly, that I had a bit of body odour. I was a young man and the fact that perspiration can cause stale odour had not occurred to me. I didn't think I needed to worry about using deodorant – I had a good wash every day, after all, and I thought underarm stuff was something that only women used. I can tell you that was one of the best pieces of advice that I've ever been given, and I've never looked back!

I have fond memories of my days at Westfield. As part of my job, I was able to attend Paddington Technical College through day release, passing the City and Guilds Higher National Certificate in the subjects I had failed at school and making up for the time that I'd previously wasted. I was slowly realising the value of hard work, and I was thrilled to be given the opportunity to learn. The absence of racism at work made me keen to repay my colleagues' trust and the time they were investing in me. I remember wishing that the teachers at school who had told me how thick I was could have seen how well I was doing.

While I was working at Westfield, I lived in digs in Neasden and would travel to and from work by bus. I earned five pounds, nineteen shillings and six pence a week; four pounds and ten shillings went on my bed and breakfast, so I wasn't left with much spending money. Given the relatively expensive cost of my lodging, which was significantly more than the going rate, it seems hard to believe that the house was owned by a Christian minister. Furthermore, if I wanted to have a bath, I'd have to pay an extra two shillings – a lot of dough at that time! However, although he got away with charging me more than he should have done, my landlord treated me well. I was grateful to him for taking me in at a time when no one else would – the only other choice I had was to live on the street.

I think one of my landlord's children tried to get in touch with me a couple of years ago – I guess they must have seen something about my police career in the news or on social media. Part of me wanted to tell her how hard her parents had made my life those years ago, but I decided not to – I wanted her to have the memory of her parents as good, kind people, and I guess they wouldn't have done it if they hadn't needed the money. Looking at the situation more rationally, I can see that we helped each other; I needed somewhere to stay, and they needed a few extra shillings to make ends meet. They may have been overcharging me, but at least they let me in during my hour of need.

I continued to attend the youth club in Muswell Hill while I was living in Neasden. Sometimes I'd miss the last bus and would end up walking home – a distance of about six miles. Thinking about it now, I guess I could have thumbed a lift, but it didn't occur to me at the time. It meant walking down the busy, smoggy North Circular for quite a lot of the way, but I wasn't frightened. I used to run some of the way, and I was always glad to save the bus fare. You need to bear in mind that I was a fit sixteen-year-old at this point, as skinny as a rake and happy to run such distances.

Every now and then, I'd walk home from work too, a distance of about five miles. I used to play a game to amuse myself. I'd walk to one bus stop and then on to the next one and then the next. I'd just carry on doing this until I thought, *Oh well – it's only a mile to my house, so I might as well continue walking!* The truth is that I was kidding myself – I barely had enough money to live on, so I had no choice but to walk everywhere.

I think it was in these days, while I was at Westfield, that I experienced most financial hardship. Eventually, I began to take a change of clothes to work every Monday and sleep on the floor of the workshop in the botany department instead of walking home to Neasden. It was OK, as I could have a shower in the building and save myself the two shillings that I'd otherwise be charged for having for a bath. Eventually, things got so bad that I couldn't afford to buy food, and I found myself living on other people's scraps. I can still remember how thrilled I was when I realised that the bins in the doctors' and professors' offices would often contain their unwanted packed lunches. When everyone had gone home, I'd go through the bins and dig out the half-eaten sandwiches, wrapped in tin foil and greaseproof paper – a feast! The experience has left me with an intolerance of waste – to this day, I can't stand to see food being thrown away. I guess living through such a difficult time gave me an insight into what life is like for people who have even less; I sometimes wish more people knew what poverty feels like.

I couldn't bring myself to tell anybody how I was living – it was my secret. I thought that one of my colleagues might have twigged that I was sleeping at the college – after all, I was always the last person in the office and I'd be there before anyone else arrived in the mornings – but no one said a thing. It might have been because they held me in high regard as a colleague and didn't want to embarrass me – I was always willing to go out of my way to assist anyone in the laboratory. I was particularly close to a professor called Tony Fogg, who was the head of the department; he wrote to me many years later to congratulate me on my police career, after reading about my achievements in the press.

I was so desperate for money that I began to go to the secretary Mrs Last's house at weekends, scrubbing her floors and tidying up her garden; she would pay me ten shillings for four hours' work, which supplemented my income. I was not afraid of work – nothing fazes you when you are young and have loads of energy, especially if you are prepared to turn your hand to anything.

It was while I'd been working at Westfield that I met my first wife, who worked in the lab with me. We were together while I was training for the police force and getting started in my career; it was only years later, when I started to work in CID, that the troubles in our marriage caused by my job came to the surface. There was nothing salacious about our divorce – it was just one of those things. It didn't work out, and we went our separate ways. The CID work I was doing at that time meant that I was hardly ever at home, and I can see now that it must have been a very stressful time for her. I think it's a common problem among police officers – the job can put a lot of pressure on a marriage.

7

Signing Up

IT WAS IN 1965, while I was nineteen years old and working at Westfield, that I saw an advert that the Metropolitan Police had placed in the *Daily Mirror* inviting people to sign up and join the police force; London needed more policemen, it said. I decided to apply, though I wasn't hopeful that it would go anywhere; sure enough, I was soon informed by letter that my application had been unsuccessful. As I would later find out, there had at this point been a lot of resistance to the idea of recruiting a Black policeman; I can't say for sure whether that had been the reason for my rejection, but they would have been aware that I was Black – I'd had to write my place of birth on the application form.

I now know that this was a political decision; the Metropolitan Police Force had for a long time been open about its opposition to the appointment of Black officers, and they were not ready to accept a Black applicant in 1965. Indeed, at a meeting of chief constables in April of that year, it was agreed that while the recruitment of ethnic minorities was acceptable in principle, the general public would probably be opposed to the idea. It sounds a lot like a cop-out to me, but I can accept that it may have been true at the time – after all, I'd experienced plenty of racial prejudice first-hand.

All this was brought to my attention in 2003 by a guy called Dr James Whitfield. While researching his PhD, he had found documents indicating that Sir Joseph Simpson, the commissioner of the Metropolitan Police between 1958 and 1968, had been reluctant to recruit a 'coloured' man into the police force; in fact, he had rejected offers of help from West Indian community leaders. (In those days, of course, 'coloured' was the polite way of saying 'Black'.) My original application, it seemed, had been turned down due to my 'temperament', a catch-all excuse that was used for the applications of everyone who was regarded as 'unsuitable'. Dr Whitfield also uncovered letters from the Home Office to the Met, where they insisted that they should recruit a Black officer, whether they liked it or not.

Undeterred – and in any case unaware of this systemic reluctance to recruit anyone from the Black community – I reapplied to the Met in 1966 and was given a preliminary interview. Little did I know that this meeting would change the course of my life. I was invited to Dean Ryle Street in Central London, where I met a representative from the Home Office – as I would later learn, the politicians were trying to persuade the Met to take its first Black officer. As far as I can remember, it felt like he was sounding me out – after all, the hiring of the first Black policeman was a momentous decision and not one to be taken lightly. I believe my application went all the way up to then Home Secretary, Roy Jenkins. How I would have loved to have been a fly on the wall at the meeting when I was being discussed!

A letter marked 'private and confidential' – dated 26 January 1967 from Mr K. A. L. Parker, a senior civil servant, to the commissioner – reinforced the Home Secretary's desire to see a coloured policeman within the Met. It goes on to say they had identified a promising candidate following an hour-long interview. That candidate? One Norwell Lionel Gumbs.

I can only imagine how the conversations went when my application was being considered. 'Who is this upstart?' 'Who does he think he is?' 'Can we trust him?' 'Has he got an agenda?' 'You realise that once we take one of that lot, we might have to take more of them?' 'Suppose he's a thicko and fails the exams – what would we do then?' 'We should think this over – let's sleep on it.' 'Perhaps he'll withdraw his application if we leave it a week or two?' 'What if we get a mass resignation of white officers?' 'If he's successful, where are we going to put him?' 'I don't think we should worry too much – he'll never last.' 'Let's give him a chance – he might change his mind when we give him a grilling at interview.' 'I reckon the other officers will make his life so miserable that he won't last, so there's no need to worry.' 'I'd bet he won't last six months, but I wouldn't like to take your money.' 'If he's successful, I'm going to resign.'

I have to laugh when I think about how the senior officers in the Met might have considered my application, although such backward opinions are clearly not very funny. However, it is important to bear in mind what was happening at the time; race riots had blighted the streets of Notting Hill in 1958 and were common all over America in the sixties, where the civil rights movement was gaining momentum. Looking back now, I can see the dilemma that the British establishment were faced with; the wrong decision could have been catastrophic.

My boss at Westfield, John Burns, knew that I'd applied for a job elsewhere, but I doubt he was very worried when he learned that I was trying to join the police. After all, there were no Black policemen at this point, so the odds that I would be successful were clearly very low. Although he didn't want to lose me from the department, he would later provide a reference that helped me join the police. I stayed in touch with him, and many years later would drive to Brighton to attend his funeral.

My fellow students at Paddington Technical College, where I attended my day release courses, also knew that I'd applied to join the police. One day, one of them, a posh lad, had a copy of the *Evening Standard* with him and read out a headline: 'London to Have First Coloured Policeman Soon'. He told me that this must mean that my application had been successful, but I said there was no way it could be me – after all, I was still waiting for a reply after my interview with the man from the Home Office.

It would later turn out that the idea had been leaked to the press, in order to gauge public opinion. I didn't dare admit the fact to anyone, but I couldn't stop myself hoping that I was the successful applicant – I just didn't want to get overexcited, in case I ended up being rejected for a second time. I need not have worried.

I first had an inkling that I was going to be accepted when I received a letter requesting that I attend an interview at Peel House on Regency Street, at the time a Metropolitan Police training school. It was nearly two years since I'd first applied, so it was a shock to think that it might actually come to something. I was asked to give the names of two referees; I put down the names of Graham Clarke, my friend from church in Bromley, and John Burns, my boss at Westfield. I've no idea what they said about me, but they must have said the right things! I believe that their names were checked by the Criminal Records Office, as were those of my neighbours. I'm not sure they go as far as checking referees these days, but at that point it was as a neces-sity – I guess there was a sensitivity around my application that required them to be particularly careful before they approved it.

I should mention that by this time I'd moved back to Bromley and was living with my mother and half-siblings, commuting to work in Hampstead each day by train, tube and bus. When I passed my driving test (my old boss from the restaurant, Alan Palmer, paid for my lessons), I saved up for a cheap car, which became my chosen mode of transport. I continued to sleep in the workshop every now and then, though – it meant that I could save money on petrol.

The day of my interview came and my heart was in my mouth, although I was fully prepared for disappointment. I sat an intelligence test alongside all the other applicants, which consisted of English, maths and general knowledge, and which I actually found quite easy – it was not dissimilar from the eleven-plus exam that I'd passed back in 1957, only for the result to be stolen from me. We then had a medical, which did not present any problems – I was very fit in those days. I can still remember the doctor telling me to cough while he cupped my testicles. As if that wasn't bad enough, he then told me to turn round, bend down and touch my toes! The only thing that made the situation less humiliating was the fact that I hadn't been singled out – everyone had to do the same.

After we'd got dressed, those of us who were successful progressed to the selection board, the final phase of the process. A uniformed police sergeant stationed outside the door wished me luck as I went in. It was a strange feeling – I couldn't remember ever being so close to a British policeman.

I'd been convinced that I was going to fail each of the previous phases in the recruitment process and remained sure that they were just humouring me; if they allowed me to get this far and only then discarded me, they would be able to say that while they had taken a Black applicant seriously, he had not met their requirements.

I entered a grand room where a dozen or so men were sitting around a long table; two or three of them were in uniform, and I expect a representative from the Home Office was also present. I sat down when they told me to do so. I cannot remember being scared, but I must have been – it was an intimating atmosphere, and I knew how much was at stake.

The panel began by telling me that I had been successful so far; I had passed the intelligence test and the medical examination. I was waiting for a 'but' to arrive, but it didn't come. They were probably doing their best to put me at ease. I guessed from the number of shiny symbols on the shoulders of those in uniform that they were mainly senior policemen. The others were in plain clothes.

Some of the men were smiling, which helped calm me. They began with a bit of small talk, before asking me why I wanted to be a policeman. I replied that it was a secure job and that I liked helping people. One of the panel then asked what they must have thought was the killer question: 'Suppose that you were on duty and a drunk called you a Black bastard – what would you do?' I answered that as a Black policeman, I was bound to get abuse, but that I would just ignore it and smile at him. This was obviously the correct answer, as it received plenty of nods of approval. I had not thought about this subject in advance; in fact, I had no idea what the correct answer was – I'd said the first thing that came into my head.

Of course, I would later learn that if certain elements were present – if his breath smelled of alcohol, his speech was slurred, his eyes were glazed or he was unsteady on his feet – he could be arrested for being drunk, but not for insulting me. As I would learn during my training, a policeman can only be insulted if the abuse comes from his own colleagues. This was something that I'd experience on many occasions.

The final question related to my reason for wanting to leave my current job. I replied that there were no opportunities for promotion, even though I'd passed exams that entitled me to attain a more senior position. With the interview over, I thanked the panel for seeing me and left the room. I remember thinking, *Thank goodness that's over – that's the last I'll ever hear from them.* If I'm being honest, I'm not sure that I would have applied a third time. I hoped, though, that the fact that I had not been put off after being rejected once would count in my favour – it showed a certain determination on my part.

I should say at this point that I cannot remember being stared at by the other applicants. That may not seem strange on the face of it, but to someone who had spent their life being in the minority, it seemed to represent progress, in a funny sort of way.

When I finally found out that my application to the police force had been successful, it was not from the police. Just as had happened before, I was at Paddington Technical College when another student in my class pointed to an article in a newspaper

– this time in his copy of the *Daily Telegraph*. 'Have you seen this?' he asked, showing me an article. The headline read, 'Coloured Man on Way to Provisionally Being Accepted as London PC'. I noted the use of the word 'provisionally', indicating that it was still not a foregone conclusion – the Metropolitan Police were clearly keen to leave themselves some wiggle room. Indeed, looking back now, I wonder if this was another example of the story being released to the press in order to sound out public opinion before the final decision was made.

At around the same time, similar articles appeared in other newspapers, some of which also printed cartoons about the story – the prospect of a Black policeman in the Met was clearly regarded as a major event. All the coverage was positive, with not so much as a hint of racism – it felt like the whole country was excited. The news even travelled across the Atlantic – an article published in one of the southern states of America was headlined 'London gets its first Negro cop'. Just as the word 'coloured' was being used in Britain, Americans had started to use the word 'Negro' in an attempt to avoid the more insensitive derivation of that word, which even now makes me wince every time I hear it. Still, although the picture in America was vastly different from north to south and some states were still segregated, there had been Black policemen for years, and even Black police federations. We were playing catch-up in the UK.

Historically speaking, the first Black policeman in Britain was a bloke called John Kent, who was born in 1795 in Carlisle. His father had been brought to this country by a slave owner and was given his liberty – a phrase that never fails to make me shudder with anger at the thought of people being treated with such contempt – before he got married and fathered a son. John joined the Carlisle City Police in 1837, but was dismissed in 1844. He was given the nickname 'Black Kent', and I bet people stared at him when he was on the beat, just like they stared at me. A wing of the St Andrews Police Treatment Centre in Harrogate, where serving and retired police officers are cared for when they are ill or injured, has recently been named in his memory – a fitting gesture that acknowledges his place in history. I was invited to attend the ceremony but politely declined – it seemed clear to me that the day should be about him, and I didn't want to distract any attention from his achievements.

There was also a biracial copper in nineteenth-century London. Robert Branford was stationed in Southwark and rose to the rank of superintendent – quite some achievement in those days, and he must have been very clever. I can only guess, but I expect his skin was lighter than mine, making him less conspicuous and helping him fit in.

Anyway, I didn't care about any of this at that point. A tingle went up my spine as my mate pointed out the article, but again I tried not to get overexcited in case I ended up being disappointed. I remember telling him that the article was probably referring to someone else, but he was convinced that it was me – and to my delight, he was proved right. In early March 1967, I received a letter from the Home Office instructing me to return to Peel House a couple of weeks later. I was over the moon and handed in my notice at Westfield – now, I felt able to get excited.

I was sorry not to have the opportunity to thank those men on the selection board who had decided to allow me to join the police force – I knew it must have been a difficult decision. I wondered if they'd taken a vote, how many of them had been in favour, and if any of them had threatened to resign. All I knew was that I was not going to let them down – I had to make the most of this opportunity.

On 28 March 1967, eleven years after I'd arrived in England, my life changed for ever. We were directed to attend Peel House at 9 a.m. but I got there early – a habit that I've never lost – arriving long before the doors opened. I remember wearing my only suit with a brand-new shirt and tie, along with a pair of black Chelsea boots I had bought especially for the occasion.

After we had been roll-called, we were welcomed into the Metropolitan Police Force by the commissioner, Sir Joseph Simpson. I couldn't help but wonder whether he was genuinely pleased that I was there or if he was addressing me through gritted teeth. After this address, I was singled out, along with four other recruits, for a photograph that was taken on the steps outside the building. One of the other new recruits whom I appeared alongside was Paul Condon, who would later become commissioner of police; the photograph appears in the first of seven scrapbooks that I have detailing my police career.

By joining the police force, I was following in the footsteps of my grandfather and my uncles who had been policemen back in the West Indies. My mum was so proud of me when she found out – I remember her taking a cutting from the local newspaper, the *Bromley and Kentish Times*, and walking up the high street proudly brandishing it, going into all the shops where we knew people and saying, 'That's my boy!' to everyone she met. It felt like a massive achievement; eleven years after arriving in the UK, the little boy from Anguilla had grown up and was the Met's first Black recruit – what a transformation!

At this point, I did not give a single thought to the possibility that I might encounter racism in my new career. I was confident that I would be readily accepted in the police force, just as I had been at Westfield College. At this point in my life, racism was something that I read about in the newspapers, but I no longer felt personally affected by it. Remember, we had no internet, mobile phones or social media – the world was very different back then. But as I was soon to discover, life as London's first Black policeman would not be at all easy.

8

Training

THE SUCCESSFUL APPLICANTS were divided into two groups, apparently at random. One group remained at Peel House, where they would complete their training; the other, which I was part of, was taken by coach to Hendon training college. Almost as soon as I got to Hendon, there seemed to be a wave of publicity relating to my recruitment. It followed me from classroom to classroom – wherever I went, there would be reporters, as well as radio and TV crews. As the trainee TS 631 Gumbs I was given the full works – the sort of treatment normally reserved for celebrities.

My story featured in all the daily newspapers, alongside lots of photographs of me looking smart in my new uniform. As a young man, I was six foot one and weighed thirteen stone – a block of muscle. I've always liked to look smart. When you had creases in your trousers, a nice shirt and walked upright, you would look as if you knew what it was all about – even if you didn't! There was press interest in my story from all over the world; I didn't mind being in the public eye, but I was glad when it calmed down a bit – all I wanted was to be a regular policeman, one of the lads.

While I was at Hendon, I remember being called into the office of the commandant, a bloke called Tommy Wall who had a fearsome reputation. First, he showed me a pile of letters of congratulation that the Met had received, but then he gestured to another pile of about twenty that were not so complimentary. In fact, they were downright racist, with the ugly words 'nigger'

and 'Black bastard' appearing in many of them, and the corres-
pondents making threats to my life if they ever encountered me
on the beat. I think the commandant showed me these disgusting letters to gauge my reaction; but if he'd hoped I would be
upset, he was going to be disappointed.

I have no doubt that some of those letters came from within
the Met; some of the anonymous writers threatened to resign if
I was posted to their station. It was obvious which ones were
sent by policemen – they were on the same teleprinter paper
that I later learned was used in all police stations. The fact that I
noticed this was an indication that I was showing detective
prowess even at this early stage in my career!

I'd never experienced racism from a policeman, but reading
these hateful letters had little effect on me. Perhaps I was so
absorbed by how I could make a success of my new career that
I could not be distracted; or maybe I was reluctant to show my
true feelings to the commandant, fearing that he would relay
any emotional response to the powers that be. After all, if I
couldn't deal with a handful of racist letters, how on earth would
I be able to deal with whatever I might encounter on the streets?
Though I was just twenty-one, I was older than my years.

The training college at Hendon looked a bit like an army
barracks. It was surrounded by fields, which have since been
replaced by blocks of modern flats. If I remember correctly, I
lived in hut number thirty-nine during my training, which was
a long dormitory with beds lining both sides. The shower and
washroom were in an adjoining building.

Our training course was to last sixteen weeks, divided into
three sections: junior, intermediate and final. During this time,
we were taught the law and had to undertake lots of practical
exercises, in which the instructors would act as stooges. You had
to pass each course to proceed to the next; if you failed any

stage, you would be put back by a week until you passed. We could not go out in the evenings – we had too much work to do – and there was little time for recreation. We had the weekends off and would head home on Friday afternoon, before returning on Sunday evening, in time for an early start on Monday.

None of my friends were in the police force, and I remember being lonely when I headed back to Bromley for the weekend, taking my washing with me. There, I would help my mother around the house and visit my friends Graham and Wendy, who still lived in Bromley. I also did a lot of studying – failing the course was not an option!

One of our tasks was to learn passages from the instruction book by heart, which we would then be tested on. Even though it was more than fifty years ago, I can remember some of the passages like it was yesterday. Among the most meaningful was Section 1, Paragraph 4: 'By the use of tact and good humour, the public can normally be induced to comply with police directions, and thus the necessity for using force with its possible consequences can be avoided.' It was a message about good policing that I would keep in my mind for my whole career.

One of my fellow trainees, a chap called Richard Bagley, who had previously been in the Rhodesian police, had an incredible photographic memory. He would spend thirty minutes reading the textbook, and fifteen hours later he'd still be able to write out all the answers exactly. How we envied him. We were also jealous of him for another reason: there was talk that he would go 'over the wall' each evening to meet up with his mates in Earls Court or to see his girlfriend before arriving back late at night, or early morning before parade.

Every morning, we would parade in front of two drill instructors, Sergeant McMoran and Sergeant Butcher, who both scared the crap out of me. I'm pretty sure they could never treat modern recruits the way they treated us!

I vividly remember being on the parade ground one

particular morning. Sergeant Butcher was inspecting us, and his face was an inch or so away from mine – all part of the act to frighten the new recruits. All of a sudden, an aeroplane flew overhead. Annoyed, he looked to the sky and shouted, 'Fuck off!' before turning back to me. I wasn't able to stop myself laughing, and soon the whole lot of us were cracking up. We were punished with an early morning parade the next day – an even earlier start than normal.

Despite the strictness of our training, some things about life at the training school were a vast improvement on what I was used to. For instance, the meals were good and plentiful – my days of living off scraps at the lab were in the past.

Some of the canteen workers at the training school were Black, and I often wondered what they thought of me. I was not singled out by any of them, or by any of the other staff; they treated me exactly the same as the other recruits, which was just the way I liked it. There were a lot of Black senior officers from other countries there for training – just as my uncles had been only a few years earlier – but we didn't really mix with them. Anyway, there was no reason why they'd have been interested in me – I was just another British bobby. There was nothing in the way of racial discrimination; nobody abused or insulted me, and the days when I had to put up with racial slurs seemed long gone. Little did I know how dramatically this was to change.

I worked hard at Hendon and passed my three exams. The pass mark for honours on the final exam was 85 per cent; I got 83.5 per cent, so I just missed out, but I was pleased to be a qualified policeman at last – Probationary Police Constable 590C. I was given my first posting: Bow Street Police Station in the heart of Covent Garden in London's West End. My beat would cover the area of London that had once been the stomping ground of the Bow Street Runners, the city's first professional police force in the eighteenth century – long before Robert Peel established the Metropolitan Police Force in 1829.

9

A New Recruit

I WENT TO BOW Street Station on 10 July 1967 with some trepidation and no idea what to expect, but I did not have to wait long to get some idea. As soon as I met my reporting sergeant, he greeted me with a snarl. 'Look, you nigger, I'll see to it that you will not finish your probation.' The significance of his remark was clear; if I didn't finish my probation, I'd be kicked out of the police.

This was the first indication that my time at Bow Street Station was going to provide a rather rude awakening. I did not allow myself to show any emotion, but found myself recalling what one of my instructors at Hendon had said when I told him where I was being posted: 'I think you'll find things a little different there.' I'd had no idea what he'd meant at the time, but now I wondered if I was starting to find out.

Let me say at the outset that I never expected to receive preferential treatment – I'd earned my place in the police force, just like anyone else, and all I wanted was to be treated the same as the other officers. However, upon my arrival at Bow Street, I immediately found myself being 'sent to Coventry'. It was just little things to start off with, but they all contributed to a feeling that I wasn't welcome there.

While I had not expected to be welcomed with open arms – I knew some officers would be shocked by the appearance of a Black police officer, and I knew that some of the racist letters Tommy Wall had received came from within the Met – I had not anticipated such a negative reaction. A couple of the police-men I'd trained with at Hendon were also posted to Bow Street; they should have put me at ease, but they were quick to side with the bullies. The only difference between us new recruits was the colour of our skin; they were white, of course, and they were accepted into the fold right away. These were people I'd chatted to and had a laugh with, who I'd regarded as mates, but as soon as we got to Bow Street, they did a complete about-turn while we were at work, refusing to have anything to do with me because they didn't want to be victimised themselves. Only when we were in the section house, the establishment for single police officers where we were boarding, did they acknowledge my existence; when we got to the station, they would revert to type and ignore me again. I don't excuse their actions, but I can understand them – we all do what we think is in our best inter-est. They wanted to be popular, and they thought ignoring me would help. For me to be popular, I'd have had to change the colour of my skin.

Only later did I find out that my colleagues had been told not to be seen talking to me by an older PC who I came to regard as the station bully. This guy was a few years older than me, and the other PCs seemed to be scared of him, yet he was a particu-lar favourite of the inspectors. He was responsible for organising the campaign of abuse that I found myself facing.

One day, another older PC told me where I should park my car; when I did exactly as he instructed, it ended up being towed away, and I had to go to the car pound at Elephant and Castle a couple of miles away to collect it. The ten shillings that I had to pay to retrieve it was a very significant sum in those days. The bullies at the station must have had a good laugh at my expense – I often wonder how many of them were in on the joke.

On other occasions, the side of my car would be scratched or its tyres would be slashed. On another day, I returned to my car to find that the keyhole had been filled with matchsticks and chewing gum. After this happened, I decided that it would be easier if I just left the car at home, where it was safe from damage, and walked to work.

Although none of my colleagues really spoke to me, the bullies did their best to make sure I was aware of their presence. I was proud to wear my uniform, but at times that became rather difficult – I'd get to the locker room to find that someone had ripped the buttons from my jacket, or I'd find it stuffed behind a cupboard, filthy from being scuffed around on the floor. In the first three years of my police career, my appointments book, instruction book, truncheon, whistle and helmet would all disappear on a regular basis; they would turn up a day or two later or be handed back to me by my sergeant, who was no doubt in on the 'joke'. I also endured many cups of tea being 'spilled' on me by colleagues who I would then spot sniggering behind their hands. I would be spat at by my fellow officers, snide remarks were the norm and I had to get used to being called 'nigger' with some regularity. All of these actions felt like blows, and I had no choice but to take it on the chin – it made me feel completely wretched.

I'd always looked forward to mealtimes when I was at Hendon, but at the station they were occasions when my isolation became particularly obvious. I vividly remember approaching the canteen one day, during my first few months at the station. I could hear laughter coming from the room – it sounded like there was some sort of party going on. However, as soon as I entered and walked up to the counter, the laughter stopped abruptly and I could feel sixty or seventy pairs of eyes boring into my front – and stabbing me in the back, too. After trying to join people at a table and get involved in a game of cards, only to find myself looking at people's backs, I gave up and sat down on my own to eat.

People often refer to 'the loneliness of the long-distance runner', but that's nothing compared to the loneliness of a Black

man in a police canteen in 1967. I wasn't desperate for intellec-
tual discussion over dinner, but a simple 'pass the salt' would
have been nice! Still, I've always tried to count my blessings; in
this case, I was glad that the catering staff were nearly all Black,
otherwise I might not have got so much as a cup of tea.

At the end of a shift, I would feel so wretched that I'd often
go back to the section house, lock myself in the bathroom and
burst into tears. To make matters worse, it soon became clear
that my enemy, the station bully, seemed to have been tasked
with making me so miserable that I would leave the force. It was
well known in the station that he disliked Black people – I heard
one of the other policemen tell the story of him opening up a
Black prisoner's head 'like a pork sausage splitting in a frying
pan'. He was clearly a most unsavoury character and not to be
messed with.

For some reason, it was decided that that I would be paired
with my nemesis for my first day on the beat. When the news
was announced, I heard some sniggering and looked over to see
him snarling in my direction. He tried to protest, but the
sergeant – the one who had greeted me with the vile comment
on my first day – was having none of it.

When the bully took me out to 'learn beats', as it was called,
he barely spoke to me and almost ran off down the road, while
I desperately tried to keep up with him. We must have looked
like an odd pair – one minute I'd be running after him and the
next he would be abruptly crossing the road, forcing cars to
brake suddenly.

It soon emerged that most of my fellow officers were reluctant to take me out; if they did agree to work with me, Bow
Street's resident bully would soon change their minds. However,
someone had to do it – learning beats was the process through
which all new recruits got the hang of police work. So rather
than having to stay out on the streets with me for eight hours,
whoever was with me would make sure he got a 'process' as

quickly as possible. This meant nicking someone for a low-level offence, whether that was a street artist painting the footway or someone going through a red light. Having found someone committing a minor crime, you could return to the station to write up their report and minimise the amount of time you spent on the streets.

Another element of the campaign of victimisation that was waged against me was that no driver would want me in his car; I lost track of the number of times when I was posted on duty in a van or car, only for the vehicle to mysteriously break down or not start, leaving me with no choice but to walk the streets. I remember one bloke even removing the rotor arm from the van to make it undriveable, so desperate was he to avoid a shift with me.

One morning, one of the veteran police constables was given the job of taking me out on the beat. Although he did not seem happy at the prospect, he knew better than to argue with the relief sergeant who had given him the order. He told me to follow him, and we walked across Covent Garden.

Nowadays, the area is mainly known for being a shopping district, popular with street performers and tourists, but in those days Covent Garden felt very different, most obviously because there was a proper market in the middle. Every night during the week there'd be a mass of lorries coming and going, with porters hauling around produce and huge crowds of people buying and selling. It might have been the middle of the night, but it would feel as busy as the middle of the day. The pubs would open at 4 a.m. to serve the market workers.

As I followed my new colleague and we walked the gauntlet of porters and salesman, there was a hush, followed by chatter once we had passed. I could tell that my 'teacher' was not happy – perhaps he was anticipating our return journey, when the stallholders would be ready for him. As we made our way back, a stallholder plucked a banana from a large stem and thrust it into my colleague's hand. 'Here's a banana for your monkey,' he said. The crowd fell silent, with everyone watching to see what would happen.

I decided that it would be best to tackle this sort of abuse head on, so I grabbed the banana from my colleague, peeled it and ate it in a couple of bites, with everyone staring at me. I then tossed the peel back to the stallholder, leaving him gobsmacked. The story spread around the market and went some way towards building my relationship with the people who worked there – though it did not seem to make my colleagues at the station hate me any less.

Despite his obvious displeasure in having to go out on the streets with me, it was the station bully who I had to thank for my first arrest. It was of a street artist who was obstructing a footway, and I can still remember his name: Robin McGillivray. When we got back to the station, having made the arrest, the bully dictated the evidence and I wrote it up in my report book.

When we later went to court, I found out that the bully had instructed McGillivray to plead not guilty – against his will – just to make things worse for me. He wanted to get me in trouble, as he thought I wouldn't be able to deal with the situation. However, his petty actions ended up working to my advantage; I was confident when giving evidence to the court and McGillivray was found guilty.

One of my most satisfying arrests as a young copper happened one night when I was flagged down by a cab driver. He told me that he had just been paid with a forged five pound note, and he seemed to think the culprit was nearby. I jumped into his cab and we soon spotted the bloke; I arrested him, hauled him into the back of the cab and took him to the station. The bloke initially claimed that he'd done nothing wrong; when I searched him, I found nothing, but noticed that he had dropped a cigarette packet on the floor of the charge room. My instinct told me to retrieve it, and I found another couple of forged fivers hidden in the packaging. As this was a criminal offence, I handed the matter to the CID. In those days, a good arrest like this should have been noted on my record of work, but you won't be surprised to learn that this did not happen.

I've been stopped by the police many times in my life, and the first time was around then, while I was stationed at Bow Street. I was returning to the section house at 3 a.m., having been to visit my mum in Bromley, when I noticed I was being followed. A police car pulled me over, and despite the officer's rudeness, I complied with his requests. I was driving a Volkswagen at the time, and he made the mistake of asking if he could look in the boot, which I unlocked from the inside. Unfortunately for him, he was so busy insulting me that he forgot that in that particular car, the 'boot' was at the front. Imagine his shock when he walked round to the back, only to find the engine. I couldn't help but laugh.

He asked to see my driving licence, so I gave it to him. He turned it over and started to look at the back to check whether I had any convictions, which I knew was against the rules. When I said, 'I don't think you're supposed to do that, are you?' he replied, 'Look, you nigger, I can do whatever I like.'

Once he'd let me go on my way, I went straight to Southwark Police Station to complain about him, but the station officer was not prepared to take my accusations seriously – he just gave me the brush off, literally throwing a pen and a pad at me instead of a statement form. When I identified myself as a police officer by producing my warrant card, he looked at me with utter disdain. There's no way that such behaviour would be tolerated these days.

I started to put a formal complaint in writing, but after a few minutes I gave up – there didn't seem to be much point when I knew it wouldn't be taken seriously. Later that morning, I relayed the incident to a senior officer at Bow Street. He promised to have a word with his equivalent at Southwark about what had happened, but he then said something disheartening that showed where his true loyalties lay: 'You can complain if you wish, but I'll be very disappointed if you do.' In the end, nothing came of it – I doubt he ever even mentioned the incident to his opposite number.

At the time, I tried to forget about what had happened and put it down to experience. How I wish now that I'd had the nous to follow through with such matters. It was the same old problem, of course – if the powers that be did not admit that there was a problem, they did not have to do anything about it. My superior officers always seemed to be telling me that I'd never make it; it was clear that they were desperate for me to fail, but that only made me keener to succeed.

Life at Bow Street was not all bad; I loved being able to interact with the public, and they generally treated me with respect. I wonder now if my accent had anything to do with this – I'd often find that white people were surprised that I sounded like I was from London rather than the West Indies.

People from the Black community, on the other hand, responded quite differently to my presence. They were generally surprised to see a Black person in a profession that had always been devoid of Black faces. While the older generation were usually welcoming, some of the youngsters in the community viewed me as a traitor. Just as is the case now, there was some resentment among Black youths who were regularly stopped and searched by the police, whether for drugs or for some other reason – what was known at the time as a 'Section 66 stop'.

Young Black people would often ask me, 'Man, why are you a policeman?' and I would always give the same answer: 'I like the life, I like meeting different people and I enjoy the job.' They would accuse me of going over to the other side, of being an Uncle Tom. In truth, I did not know what this phrase meant; when I looked it up, I found out that it is used to describe a Black person who is subservient to white people. I completely disagreed with this assessment of my behaviour; I felt like I was doing what I could to help other Black people – I had no intention of being subservient to anyone!

Maybe Black people viewed me with suspicion because the way I spoke was not typical for a West Indian. However, I wonder now if the police missed a trick by not posting me in a Black area like Brixton or Notting Hill – I might have been able to educate youngsters from that community. I loved the thought that people might regard me as a role model; on one occasion when I was out on the beat, a Black bus driver stopped his bus in the middle of the Strand and asked me what life was like in the police. I couldn't bear to tell him about the bullying – at this point, I thought that if more Black people signed up, I'd feel less alone – so I painted a very rosy picture. I later found out that he'd joined up – I was clearly an effective recruiting tool.

Although I was generally treated well by the public, Covent Garden Market did present a few problems. However, I think my detractors were probably disappointed that I got on well with most of the market porters. In fact, once I'd worked at Bow Street for a little while, I didn't have to pay for any fruit or vegetables – I befriended some of the porters and stallholders and they looked after me, giving me as much produce as I wanted. All the other officers received similar perks, but it meant a great deal to be treated in the same way as everyone else. Their warmth provided me with a refuge, in stark contrast to the station, where I was under constant pressure; it was such a relief that it felt like manna from heaven.

Another time, after my probation, I was in Covent Garden Market with a rookie officer and was teaching him beats. He was posher than me and spoke quite properly, so he said to a suspect, 'Excuse me, old boy. Can you tell me what you've got there?' The bloke he was talking to was completely nonplussed and just looked at him, so I said, 'Oi! Empty your fucking bins!' It turned out that the man was wanted for possession of stolen goods. I'd told my colleague who to stop – it was another example of how, as an officer on the beat, you'd get a feeling that something wasn't right.

One of the biggest fruit and veg firms in the market was called Nash and Austin, and I can remember the owner letting me sit in his E-Type Jaguar. I was particularly close to one of the firm's workmen, a chap who was known as 'Big Harry'. He must have weighed about twenty-five stone, and he was so strong that he could throw a half-hundredweight (about 25 kg) sack of potatoes into his van with ease. After Harry's death, I stayed in touch with his wife, occasionally taking groceries to her at home in Peckham, South London.

The locals at the market were not always so friendly. I remember being on the beat there one night when I called for the van to pick me up after I had arrested a drunk who had become abusive. Even though I was barely 200 yards away from the station, the van never came. I somehow managed to turn the situation to my advantage, subduing the assailant and carrying him back to the station on a trolley I'd borrowed from a porter. When I got back to Bow Street, the van was in the yard with the engine running and the driver, the same bloke who had organised the hate campaign against me, was laughing with his mates as they relaxed and drank cups of tea. Their faces turned to thunder when they noticed me. They probably hoped that I would be getting my head kicked in, and they were annoyed to see that I had sorted out the problem without their help.

As my troubles at the station continued, I was grateful that I'd made a lot of friends on the beat, and would often get invited into people's houses for cups of tea. In my eyes, this was the essence of good policing; I got an insight into what the public were thinking, and they got a policeman whom they could trust. The other advantage for me was that it helped me make friends at a time when I felt isolated from my colleagues. The other coppers would not have enjoyed seeing how much the community appreciated me.

I often used to play football and cricket with some of the local kids from the neighbourhood's Peabody flats, a late-nineteenth-century estate that had been built as part of the effort to clear London's slums and was now home to council tenants. I remember hitting a ball and breaking a window of one of the flats. We all scarpered, and thankfully the kids didn't dob me in. Such was my friendship with them that when the Met's PR department wanted some photos of me in the local community, the Peabody estate was the obvious place to go. My favourite photograph is one of a group of young children laughing as they tried on my helmet, while I kneeled down so that I was at their level. As it happened, I knew all the kids and their parents by name – they were the same people who would regularly invite me into their houses, which was a huge help in maintaining my sanity. I didn't need to go to the station canteen, to be stared at and insulted, when I had so many friends on the beat.

Lorries would bring produce to the market at Covent Garden from all over the country. One morning, I encountered a small girl on one such vehicle, sitting on the back of it and guarding her dad's fruit and veg. She can't have been much older than eight. I knew her dad and he had asked me to look after his daughter while he was buying some more produce. I was simply talking to her when someone spotted us and took a photo; once again it ended up in the newspapers.

The press interest in my career was so extreme at that point that everything I did seemed to become a news story; it felt like if I accidentally belched, the headline the next day would be 'London's First Coloured Policeman Breaks Wind While on

Duty'! It's worth noting that at this point, the headlines all referred to me as 'London's First *Coloured* Policemen'; later on, this would become 'London's First *Black* Policeman', a reflection of how times were changing. The word coloured is now regarded as an insult, but it felt far preferable to some of the things I would be called during my career.

10

Doing the Job

THE WEST END, where I spent my early years in the force, was always very busy in the late 1960s – just as it is now. In the mornings, huge crowds of people would get off the train at Charing Cross Station and walk down to Trafalgar Square or get on buses to take them to work. The queues at bus stops could be fifty yards long, but the crowds were generally friendly.

In those days, it wasn't unusual to see men on the streets wearing bowler hats. I remember standing outside the South African embassy one night, struggling to stay awake – some night shifts were so boring that you'd almost fall asleep standing up, just for a couple of seconds. It was about three o'clock in the morning when I saw this bloke walking towards me from Upper St Martin's Lane, heading towards Whitehall. He was wearing a bowler hat and carrying a briefcase, and I just didn't like the look of him – don't ask me why. I said, 'Excuse me, sir – can you tell me where you're going?' He said, 'I'm just going home.' I said, 'What's in the briefcase? Can I have a look please?' He opened it up, to reveal that it was full of silver – it turned out that he'd stolen it from a big house in the area. It was worth thousands. I arrested him; someone came to take my place and I took him to the station, where he was handed over to CID. He'd come quietly, but he didn't have any choice – if he started giving me any trouble, I would have said, 'Look, you can either open your bag here, or we can go to the station and do it.'

I can't tell you exactly why I stopped him – it's what we would refer to as 'reasonable suspicion', which relates to the time, the place and the circumstances. If it was three o'clock in the morning and someone was hanging around the back of a shop, you might think their behaviour was a bit out of character. Working on the beat would give you a good sense of when people looked like they were behaving shiftily or when they were up to no good – after a while, it was a feeling that just became second nature.

In my uniformed days, the 'early turn' shift was between 6 a.m. and 2 p.m., the 'late turn' would be 2 p.m. to 10 p.m. and night duty would run from was 10 p.m. to 6 a.m. If you were ever late for early turn, the sergeant would say, 'You're not late for early turn – you're just early for late turn.' You'd have to go home and come back again at two.

One of my favourite parts of life on the beat was point duty, which we would be posted to during the morning and evening rush hours. We'd wear white gauntlets on our arms, which made us visible to motorists and pedestrians. The points we controlled were on the Strand, at the junctions with Duncannon Street and Villiers Street, and opposite Charing Cross Station. You'd often see the same people on the streets – the local characters in the West End – and you got to know them. Some of them used to call me Mr Roberts, and I developed quite a rapport with them.

I don't suppose this duty would be popular these days; the nature of the work left you with no choice but to inhale the fumes of the buses, the black cabs and cars driving along one of London's busiest roads. Back then, however, I enjoyed the responsibility – I always relished the tremendous sense of power that came with directing the traffic. If I pointed to a car, the driver had no choice but to stop, although you'd always try to dispatch stationary traffic without unnecessary delay. I also enjoyed how point duty allowed me to interact with members of the public, which was especially welcome at a point when I was being shunned by my fellow officers at the station.

While I was on point duty one day, directing traffic at the junction with Villiers Street, an elderly lady came up to me and struck up a conversation. Some of my colleagues would probably have dismissed her as a nutter and ushered her away, but I decided to remove my gauntlets and went to the side of the road to have a chat. It soon became clear that she was very lonely – she had no family and just wanted someone to talk to.

After we'd talked for fifteen minutes, she said, 'Thank you for listening to me – our policemen never normally do that.' I reflected on these words once my shift had finished and found myself wondering whether she found me easier to talk to than a white policeman. Whether that was the case or not, providing a listening ear for the lonely and unfortunate members of the community is surely a big part of the role of an officer.

I was on the beat one day near the Strand and I met the eyes of this bloke. He looked at me and said, 'It's Noel, isn't it?' I corrected him and we got chatting. His name was Mr Green, and he'd been caretaker at Haverstock Comprehensive School when I was a pupil. It turned out that he was now caretaker at St Clement Danes Primary School, on Drury Lane, and he invited me over for a cup of coffee. Soon, I was going there regularly, to see him and have a break during a shift – it's what we'd call a 'tea hole', a place where we'd have a rest before going back on the beat. I preferred to walk through the buildings because when people saw a copper, in the old days, they'd feel happier and safer. When I got divorced from my first wife, Mr Green's stepdaughter Wendy was at a loose end, and it turned out that we got on pretty well. The rest, as they say, is history – we've been together for forty-six years.

11

I'm a Policeman, Not a Politician

I WAS MAINLY DEALING with petty crime in the late 1960s, but I did have one brush with a notorious character from London's gangland. I was standing around at Bow Street Magistrates' Court one day when I noticed a little chap on the other side of the waiting room. He stood out from the crowd – he was dapper and well groomed, with a little handkerchief in his front pocket. It was Ronnie Kray. At this time, he and his twin brother Reggie were in their pomp and known throughout London. He introduced himself to me, and I remember that he stunk of Brut cologne. I asked what he was in for, and he said, 'They've fucking got me for going through a red light.' He was annoyed, because after everything he'd done, he'd been nicked for something as insignificant as going through a poxy red light. The Kray twins controlled much of the East End, while the Richardsons were the family who ruled over South London; the two gangs argued over the West End because that's where the money was – that's where the clashes happened.

Soho in the sixties was where everything seemed to happen, but it wasn't on my beat – I covered Covent Garden, the Strand and Lincoln's Inn Fields. I remember nicking a famous actor – who will remain nameless – who was appearing in a play at the Strand Theatre. He went through my signal, so I stopped and reported him. Then he said, 'If you nick me, I won't send any more free tickets to the station' – in those days, the theatres would send any spares to the station. I nicked him, but needless to say he never ended up in court.

There might have been more serious corruption, but if there was it was well above my pay grade. There was some low-level corruption – looking the other way when something went on, for instance – but it would work as a sort of 'tit for tat'. We had to get information somehow; remember that we didn't have CCTV in those days, so we might choose to let a small misdemeanour go in order to get information about a bigger crime.

Back then, every good CID officer had an informant – someone who would give you information in exchange for payment from Scotland Yard. I dealt with a lot of them in my undercover work.

When I was on the beat on my own, I would sometimes have to stand at a fixed protection post for an entire eight-hour shift, with a forty-five-minute break to get some grub. This was a type of posting that every policeman had to endure now and then. There were two main 'fixed posts' during my time at Bow Street – South Africa House and Rhodesia House, now the Zimbabwean Embassy. Both these buildings were associated with racist regimes – this was the height of apartheid in South Africa, while Rhodesia was governed by Ian Smith, an ardent advocate of white rule. When I was posted outside them, people – who were generally Black – would come up and ask me if I liked standing outside and protecting them. I would calmly reply, 'I'm just doing my job – I'm a policeman, not a politician.'

I remember being on point duty outside Rhodesia House one night and this bloke, obviously the worse for wear, said, 'Can you nick me? I want a bed for the night.' I said, 'I can't do that – you've got to do something wrong.' 'Like what?' he said. 'Like break a window.' So he went away, got a brick, broke a window and I arrested him. He must have been pretty desperate, but he got a bed for the night. When he went to court, it turned out that he was a prolific criminal and he was sent to prison.

At no time during this duty did I question whether I should be standing outside the buildings of such distasteful regimes, even though there was definitely something about being there that felt uncomfortable. There was no way that I could imagine saying to my sergeant, 'Sorry, Sarge – I don't feel like working there today.' It's important to remember that guarding an embassy does not in any way imply an acceptance of that country's policies.

Anyway, I did not mix my job with politics – after all, I was just an ordinary copper doing my job. It might sound corny, but it really was as simple as that – I was more conscious of the importance of doing a good job than of the political conse-quences. If you do the right thing, you'll always be supported. Throughout my career I tried to be a good, fair copper. And when it came to fixed post duties, I generally enjoyed them because I could interact with members of the public; at the station, I was a lot more lonely.

One of the things that I found surprising about being posted outside the South African embassy was that when I needed to use the bathroom, I was allowed into the building – which felt slightly ironic in the age of apartheid! I also befriended the cultural attaché of the embassy; he came to my house on more than one occasion and I would go up to see him in his office on the first floor of the embassy. He was a nice person who clearly did not believe in his country's political system, but I wonder what his colleagues made of our friendship.

One of the times when I felt my principles being put to the test was when I was on duty outside the Rhodesian embassy on the day that Ian Smith's regime hanged three Black men.

My reporting sergeant, the one who had made the racist remark to me on my first day at Bow Street, posted me there for four hours – his idea of a joke. I was quickly withdrawn when there was a demonstration by a hundred or so students and twenty MPs, as well as the solicitor for two of the hanged men. The press was out in force and my presence was becoming a focus of attention, rather than the poor men who had met their end under such a dreadful regime. The sergeant's decision to send me there had backfired on him big time.

Many years later, I was asked to comment on the decision by the Met to remove a Muslim firearms officer from duty outside the Israeli embassy – the situation was seen to have parallels with the one I'd been placed in. It was suggested that the officer had asked to be removed due to his family's connections to Lebanon, a country that was under attack from Israeli troops. I remember thinking at the time that if the officer had made that request, he was out of order, and I still do – you don't get to choose which jobs suit you. I was also annoyed with his senior officers – they should have listened to his concerns, but withdrawing him from the embassy was not the right thing to do, not least because it would set a precedent.

I can only imagine the furore there would have been had I refused to stand outside either the South African or Rhodesian embassy. I expect I'd have been given my P45 for refusing to obey a lawful order, and quite right too – in those days, you had no choice but to comply with all orders straight away and without question. I may have been posted outside these embassies out of malice, but guarding them was part of my job as a policeman and I wasn't going to let anyone tell me that my ethnicity made me unsuitable. Nothing could be harder than having to stand outside the Rhodesian embassy on that day, but I wasn't at any greater risk than my colleagues, and there was no way that I wanted to receive preferential treatment. It was, without doubt, one of the toughest days during my long career – but I was determined to stand alongside my colleagues and do my job.

★   ★   ★

Another memorable moment in the early days of my police career came when I was on duty at the famous demonstration against the war in Vietnam outside the American embassy in Grosvenor Square on 17 March 1968. Young people had become a lot more politically engaged than they had been even a decade earlier. At that time, if you stopped someone, they would all say, 'I know my rights.' People would hand out cards to people, instructing them to give their name and date of birth if they were stopped by the police, and nothing else.

Due to the size of this particular demonstration, police had been drafted in from various other parts of the Met. By the end of the day, there were more than 200 arrests, while eighty-six people were treated for injuries. Fifty people, including around twenty-five police officers, were taken to hospital.

Earlier in the day, there had been a big rally in Trafalgar Square, with thousands of people turning out to demonstrate against the war. They were addressed by speakers including the actress Vanessa Redgrave, who would later deliver a petition to the embassy. A few hundred of us surrounded the embassy, standing shoulder to shoulder to prevent the crowds reaching the entrance.

The mood at the Trafalgar Square rally had initially been good-natured, but it all started to kick off when the protesters marched to the embassy. The police ordered the crowd to back off, but they refused, so mounted officers were sent in to try to take control. The demonstrators managed to break through our ranks and make it as far as the lawn of the embassy, where they did a lot of damage, tearing up fences and uprooting a hedge.

During ugly scenes that were closer to a running battle than the peaceful demonstration that had been planned, we had stones, lumps of earth, firecrackers and smoke bombs thrown at us, leaving us struggling to keep control. There were serious injuries to several of my colleagues – one officer was treated for a spinal injury and another for a neck injury. Another of my colleagues had his hat knocked off and was struck on the back of the head with the pole from a banner as he clung to his horse for dear life.

The next day, the Labour MP Peter Jackson told *The Times*, 'I was particularly outraged by the violent use of police horses, who charged into the crowd even after they had cleared the street in front of the embassy.' He announced that he would be asking a question in the House of Commons about what he referred to as 'police violence'.

Jackson was entitled to his opinion, of course, but I think he'd have felt slightly differently if he'd been one of the officers who had found themselves facing a crowd of some 10,000 angry demonstrators! I was also irritated that he'd failed to mention that the lines of police held firm, even while we were being pelted with rocks, sticks and flour bombs. The demonstrators, although claiming to be motivated by a desire for peace, had few qualms about putting our lives at risk. They had also brought loads of marbles with them, which they threw on the road in front of the horses, endangering both the animals and their riders. They can't have been animal lovers, as they weren't at all bothered about the untold injuries they caused to the horses.

During the riot, I had been stationed in a line of the officers at the bottom of the steps leading to the embassy. I don't know whether there was any truth in the rumour, but we heard that there were armed American marines within the building's entrance hall; apparently, if the police lines were breached and the demonstrators managed to get inside, the marines would have taken over and dealt with the situation.

I was involved in policing another politically delicate event a couple of years later. At the anti-apartheid demonstrations that were held at the rugby match between the Barbarians and South Africa at Twickenham on 31 January 1970, I was one of many officers who 'lost' their helmets.

The South African rugby team was one of the best teams in the world at the time; they came to Britain expecting to win all their games, but they returned home after four difficult months, with the whole tour having been disrupted by anti-apartheid protests. Furthermore, they had failed to win a single one of their four test matches.

It was a rude awakening for most of the South African squad, who were young men with little experience of the world away from their own country. In addition, their own media did not cover the huge international opposition to their country's racist political regime. The games were only able to go ahead with a wall of policeman to prevent pitch invaders; sometimes barbed-wire barriers were constructed. The trip was dubbed 'the tour that changed international sport'; the public response to the tourists' presence in Britain was so strong that a ban of South African sports teams soon followed.

I was on duty at Twickenham that day, along with many other officers. I can vividly remember standing in a line of policemen behind a barrier, doing everything we could to prevent the demonstrators invading the pitch. We were facing a hostile crowd who were frothing at the mouth and venting their anger at us – the police – for being there. What they didn't seem to realise was that all we were doing was preventing lawlessness and disorder – it was not as if we were endorsing apartheid!

Among the disruptive things the protestors insisted on doing, one of the most annoying was that they would reach out and grab our helmets, before ripping out the lining and taking the badge and the rose from the top. They would then kick the helmets around a bit before chucking them back at us – they wouldn't dare leave the ground with them, as they would be too big to conceal.

A few of us who were positioned in the front line saw what was happening, so we removed our helmets and placed them behind the police lines, out of the protestors' reach. The next day, I was in the press once again – my photo was on the front of the *Sunday Express*, in which I was identified as 'a coloured policeman who has lost his helmet'. I think the point they were trying to make by printing the photo was that a Black police-man was facing up against anti-apartheid demonstrators. The protestors felt they were fighting for my rights, yet I appeared to be against them. What they didn't realise, however, was that I just felt like any other policeman doing his job – the only differ-ence was that I just so happened to be Black.

If you look at the picture, you'll see that my expression is completely deadpan. I can remember the moment when it was taken, and I was not thinking much – I was simply doing my job. It was not the right time for a laugh and a joke, and it would have been completely inappropriate to engage in any sort of political discussion with the protestors, even if that was what they wanted. And thanks to my quick thinking, I was able to leave with my helmet intact!

The next time I policed an anti-apartheid demonstration, it was a very different story. I was part of a team of five officers who were asked to police a group of fifty clergymen who were holding a twenty-four-hour-long vigil outside the South African embassy in August 1971. They were protesting at the detention of the Dean of Johannesburg, who had been arrested and held without charge by the notoriously secretive South African National Defence Force. Needless to say, it was a peaceful demonstration. My photograph once again appeared in the press, taken at a moment when I was in deep discussion with the organiser Dr Ambrose Reeves, the Assistant Bishop of Chichester, who had been expelled from South Africa ten years before when he was Bishop of Johannesburg.

Crowd control sometimes involved working at events that were far less confrontational. In May 1970, I helped at the premiere of the Beatles film *Let It Be*. Thousands of fans mobbed Piccadilly Circus in the hope of catching a glimpse of the Fab

Four. However, even at this event, I found myself a focus of press attention, the *Daily Mail* reporting:

> There is something richly good-humoured about this picture of PC Norwell Roberts holding back a crowd of Beatlemaniacs [. . .] right in the front line, cheerfully protecting the peace – for people can get hurt, even in the friendly matches [. . .] Most of us worry about the problems of immigration. But it is worth giving a thought to how much we already owe to coloured nurses, bus conductors, doctors and the rest. Is it fancy to imagine their fresh outlook lends an extra touch of gaiety to our daily round?

Being written about in this way made me feel good. Despite the abuse I'd suffered from my colleagues, I felt like I'd already been accepted by the vast majority of the public; now it seemed that the newspapers were coming round to the idea, too.

One of the advantages of being stationed at a Central London police station was that we would be on duty outside London theatres when the Queen or other members of the royal family attended film premieres or theatre productions. On one such evening I was given a megaphone to summon the cars of the distinguished guests, as they were parked some distance from the theatre.

One of my colleagues asked me to summon the car of a Lord Jellicoe. I must have been in a jovial mood, so I decided to have a bit of fun and bellowed, 'The carriage for Lord Jellybaby!' I hastily corrected myself, but the theatregoers and a few of my colleagues – as well as Lord Jellicoe himself – all found this very amusing. I suppose my poker face saved my bacon. As on many other occasions, being able to laugh at myself helped me cope with what could be a very stressful work life.

12

On My Own

ONE AFTERNOON DURING my CID (Criminal Investigation Department) attachment – a stage in my probationary period that involved spending a few weeks working with plain-clothes officers who worked on more serious crimes – the detective chief inspector at the station called me into a corner of an office to talk to him. I thought he was going to tell me something important and eagerly ran up to him. He looked around, as if to establish the coast was clear, before whispering in my ear, 'Go and get the fucking teas, son.' I found this quite amusing, and we had a good laugh – it was a nice change to feel like I was in on the joke for once.

I didn't feel like I was being targeted by this DCI – he was just like that. He was from the older generation, which typically had traditional views about how the police hierarchy worked, but he was in the CID, and they tended to be very different from uniformed officers. There were no doubt a few racists there, but the problem seemed to be less overt than among uniformed officers – unless I was becoming better at ignoring it! I suspect the truth is a combination of both things; as I progressed in my career, more officers began to accept me, leaving the haters in a minority.

Although I felt like one of the gang at certain times, there were other occasions when racism was hard to ignore. One memorable incident occurred at around the same time, during my CID attachment, when I was asked to ring up a police station in South London to make enquiries about a Black suspect, only for the police officer who answered to say, 'We don't have any niggers fitting that description.' I thanked him for his trouble and comforted myself by thinking that the joke was actually on him – he had no idea to whom he had addressed his racist reply. In those days, such racist attitudes were standard among many officers – I wonder what he would have thought if he'd known that he was talking to a Black person.

All new police officers are reported on by a sergeant and an inspector throughout their service, but the first two years after joining are the most crucial; if a policeman doesn't show his capabilities in that time, he can be dismissed. I was certain that whatever I went through at Bow Street, there was no way that I was going to fail on that account.

Obviously, I had some very antagonistic colleagues to deal with, which didn't help; I was constantly having to fight against a barely concealed feeling that lots of my fellow officers would rather I wasn't there. When I found that some anonymous person had ripped my pocket book in half, I just stuck it back together with Sellotape. On countless other occasions my reports were ripped in half, and I always did the same thing and acted as if nothing had happened – complaining wouldn't have got me anywhere.

It was obvious that things were just not working out with my reporting sergeant and inspector, and the fact that my records of work were always being downgraded was a major part of the problem. I only learned afterwards that the sergeant had again said openly that he planned to do everything he could to get me out of the police force as soon as possible.

Allow me to explain how he went about undermining my work. If, for instance, I had made a dozen arrests, twenty summonses and a large amount of stops in a three-month period, he would doctor my report so that it showed just a few arrests and summonses. In this way, he planned to make sure that I would be drummed out within the first two years due to a poor work record.

However, he did not stop there – he also observed in his report on me that I 'kept myself to myself in the canteen, did not mix with other officers, was a bit of a loner and did not get on with members of the public'. He went as far as to say that he didn't think I would last a year – in his charming words, 'He would never make a policeman as long as he had a hole in his arse.' Well, after thirty years' loyal service and without any radical changes to my anatomy, I think I can safely say that I proved him wrong!

After I'd put up with this sort of treatment for about a year, with his reports about me being full of blatant lies, I requested a meeting with the chief superintendent, at which I suggested that I thought there was a 'clash of personalities' – a polite way of saying that my reporting sergeant and inspector were both complete and utter racists. Once my complaint was taken seriously and I was allocated a different reporting sergeant and inspector, it was no surprise that my reports started to improve and I began to feel a little better about myself.

But even with a new reporting line, the racism that I found myself facing within the Met continued. On one particularly sad day, I was on duty outside the Royal Opera House when a panda car went past, and as it did the driver shouted 'Black cunt!' at me at the top of his lungs out of the open window.

As the vehicle screeched past, I could hear the other two policemen in the car laughing. I felt wretched, especially when I noticed that passing members of the public who had heard me being abused were walking on by, their heads lowered. It would have been nice if one of them had gone into the police station, which was just across the road, and made a complaint, but I guess such behaviour would have been unusual in those days

– society was not ready to make that step. In any case, even now, as shocked as many people would be to hear a police officer using such disgraceful language, I doubt many people would be brave enough to step in and do something about it.

One of the most important things that we had been taught at training school was that 'idle and silly remarks were unworthy of note and should be disregarded', but surely I shouldn't have been expected to turn the other cheek when faced with such abuse. I walked across the road to the police station and went up to the chief superintendent's office, where I told him what had happened. But instead of being sympathetic, he just said dismissively, 'Well, what do you expect me to do about it?'

When he reacted like this, I just thought to myself, 'I've lost – I've allowed them to get under my tough outer skin.' Until then, I'd always managed to hide my upset with a smile, but I didn't feel like I could do it anymore – I'd already been through so much. I just said, 'Nothing, sir' and left the room, before dashing back to the section house and crying so much that I thought the bath would fill up with my tears. The haters had won again, and there was no one for me to turn to – I was on my own. That was, without doubt, one of the lowest points of my whole career.

I was struggling to cope and very short of friends. Fortunately, at some point during my time at Bow Street I got to know a guy called Bob Broeder, who worked for a newspaper firm in Covent Garden. He became a confidant, a shoulder to cry on at a very difficult time. The strange thing is that I can't remember telling him about everything that I was going through, but I must have done – when we saw each other many years later, he was able to recall some of the traumatic stories I'd told him. He could probably tell at the time that I'd just been putting on a brave face.

As well as Bob, I was also able to speak to my friends Graham and Wendy Clarke. I don't remember the conversations I had with them when I was at my lowest ebb, but they do! Many years later, Graham said to me, 'You used to come to us and tell us about the terrible time you had down there.' Again, it seems like my subconscious mind has tried to block out the nastiness. I've no idea how that happened – I guess it's a question for a psychologist.

After the incident outside the opera house, I recall wondering if it was worth putting up with all the pain that seemed to be inevitable if I was to remain in the police. I felt like there wasn't anyone in the force who I could talk to about how I was feeling. I had plenty of opportunities to blow the lid on the maltreatment I was suffering – I was summoned to Scotland Yard on more than one occasion, and I remember sitting in the office of the deputy assistant commissioner who was in charge of recruitment. He asked me if I had any problems, but I lied and told him that everything was fine. I'm not sure whether he believed me; I remember him pausing, as if he wanted to ask me some more questions on that subject. I smiled at him, trying to convince him that I was happy and doing well. This was not true, of course – I just didn't want to be seen as a failure.

It may have been a period that I'd rather forget, but there are some aspects of it that I'm keen to remember. I always want to keep the memory of how difficult it was, so I can appreciate the journey I've been on. Many years later, I found myself wondering whether I could have done things differently. I'd first chosen to speak publicly about the racism I'd experienced in an interview with the *Guardian* in 1986, when I stated that racial prejudice existed in the police force and that anyone who denied it was lying. This was a big moment for me; until that point, I'd made a point of doing everything I could to avoid criticising the police force in public. In the article, I recounted some of my experiences from my Bow Street days and said that I was beginning to understand why Black youths in areas of London like Brixton and Hackney had such a mistrust of the police.

The previous year, police relationships with the community in London had been damaged by two tragic events. On 28 September 1985, police officers had burst into the Brixton home of Cherry Groce, a thirty-seven-year-old Black lady. They were looking for her son but mistakenly shot her, leaving her paralysed from the waist down. Just a week later, police in Tottenham broke down the front door of Cynthia Jarrett, causing her to die of heart failure. Both incidents led to riots and damaged the image of the Met – especially among the Black community – but in my interview I stopped short of suggesting there was institutional racism or that senior officers were turning a blind eye. I'm not sure what I was expecting, but nothing changed following my interview. I probably shouldn't have been surprised.

In 1999, when the Macpherson Report into the police investigation into the murder of Stephen Lawrence was published, numerous newspapers contacted me for comment, leading to an article with the headline, 'In a Way It's My Fault, Says Black Policeman'. That was a misinterpretation of what I said – I had felt as if I was somehow to blame, but I also knew that was certainly not the case. What I said was that I ought to have been more vociferous in my condemnation of the police officers who had treated me so very badly. However, even if I had spoken up more loudly about the bullying I suffered, what difference would that have made? It certainly wouldn't have done anything to stop the racist and violent white youths from attacking an innocent Black teenager on the street more than twenty years later. As for the police force, no matter what I'd said back in the late 1960s, the racist and corrupt elements that existed within the Met would still have been there. I was trying to speak up by this point, but no one was listening.

Looking back now, my rejection when I first applied to join

the police in 1965, when the powers that be decided that 'it was not the right time' to accept a Black officer, seems to provide something of a parallel with what happened all those years later. Back then, the Met had not been ready to accept a Black officer, just as the Macpherson Report had proven that they had not been willing, three decades later, to do anything about the institutional racism that existed within the force – at neither time was there sufficient will for change. Anyway, even if I *had* spoken out early in my police career, it would have made no difference. I think some people expected me to buckle under the pressure and in the face of all the vicious treatment I received, but that wasn't me – I was made of stronger stuff. I was quiet on the outside but I was as hard as nails underneath – and I'm glad I was, because it helped me cope.

I did not think then – and nor do I think today – that the killers of Stephen Lawrence could have been convicted earlier if I'd done anything different way back in the sixties or seventies. It was only because of an amazing effort from Stephen's mother, Doreen, that justice was eventually done. She recruited some hard hitters to back her protests and gained the support of the media. She would later receive a damehood for her endeavours, and rightly so. While I do wish that I'd spoken out more about racism during my early years, it would not have made the slightest difference – it was not 'the right time'.

During another visit to Scotland Yard, I was asked by the deputy assistant commissioner whether it was my ambition to go to Bramshill, a police college for accelerated promotion. I told him that I was not interested in doing that – I just wanted to be a good copper. I wonder now if I should have tried to climb the ladder – maybe if I'd risen to a more senior rank, I'd have been better placed to effect change.

13

A Public Figure

'WHO WAS THE first man to walk on the moon?' a reporter once asked me. 'Neil Armstrong,' I replied. 'And who was the second?' she went on, only for me to confess that I had no idea. 'I rest my case,' she replied. 'People always remember the first, but they rarely remember the second.' I'd asked her why she was so keen to write about me, and her response said it all: I was *the first*, and rightly or wrongly, that made me special.

I had to get used to appearing in the press and on television. After all, everything I did was news because I was the first Black police officer to do it. The Met knew I could be trusted to say the right thing and not slag off the police force. Some people criticise me for that now, but it's easy to do so with the benefit of hindsight – they should consider how tough things were back in the sixties and seventies.

If there was an incident and I was there, you could rest assured that my picture would appear in the paper. Sometimes the article would not have anything to do with me personally – it might be about the policing of a National Front march or a television programme on race relations – but there I would be. In fact, it became a bit of a standing joke that I got more publicity than the commissioner – it sometimes felt like I was one of the most famous Black men in London at the time. The press seemed to follow me everywhere. Lots of people were hoping that I would slip up, which meant that I had to be very careful.

Some of the stories were made to seem more light-hearted than was actually the case; when I was photographed lifting an older gentlemen's hat at Bow Street Magistrates' Court, for instance, the headline was 'Keeping It Under His Hat?' In reality, I was part of the security detail at the trial of individuals who were accused of being involved in bombings in London carried out by the IRA, and one of my duties was to stand outside the court, searching everyone who entered. It seemed perfectly reasonable to assume that someone entering the court's public gallery might have had some sort of device concealed under his hat; one of my colleagues even searched a pram with a baby in it! The press may have thought my actions were funny – I can see that they created a good headline – but I was just doing my job.

One of my favourite press cuttings from this part of my career features a photo of me carrying an elderly lady named Dorothy Wilson down a busy street. She had fallen over while getting on a bus on the Strand with several bags of shopping, twisting her ankle in the process. The headline in the *Daily Telegraph* was 'The Strong Arm of the Law', while the paper quoted me as saying 'A cop's gotta do what a cop's gotta do.' In actual fact, I had not been asked for a comment, and nor did I have the energy to say anything – as I would later find out, the lady weighed fourteen stone, and that didn't include the weight of her shopping!

A few years later, at around the time of the Notting Hill Carnival, the same photograph appeared on the front cover of *Private Eye*. The headline was 'Notting Hill, Officer, and Be Quick About It'. I'm not sure why they used my picture, but I guess they just thought it was a funny image!

Sometimes it was not just me who made the headlines; my presence would occasionally lead to criminals getting more attention than they would have otherwise received. One guy called David Patterson took exception to me removing him from Charing Cross Hospital at the request of the nursing staff.

When we got outside, he headbutted me. I managed to restrain him with a few well-placed strikes and arrested him. The police van turned up and we took him back to Bow Street, where he was charged. He was tried at the crown court, where he was found guilty and was fined £100 and received a suspended sentence, as well as a star appearance in several newspapers. It was my involvement that made the story newsworthy – the headline was 'Man Who Assaulted London's First Coloured Policeman is Fined £100'. Even changing my surname by deed poll to Roberts attracted a piece in *The Times* diary pages, something that was generally reserved for London socialites.

I was no saint as a police officer, and I had my share of complaints. Many of them were frivolous, but a couple were deserved. I didn't worry too much about them – after all, there was a saying in the Met at the time: 'If you do nothing, you'll never get a complaint.' There was some truth in this idea – if you stayed under the radar and kept your head down, you would never get a complaint, but nor would you achieve very much. The good thing about complaints was that you had the chance to learn from them, but it was always a bit of a relief to be handed a 163A form, meaning that the complaint had been determined to be unsubstantiated.

One of the complaints against me that *was* substantiated related to a time when I was reported for speeding on my way home from work. I was driving at 35 mph in an area with a 30 mph limit. The traffic officer who reported me was only doing his job, but he had a glint in his eye, as if he knew who I was and couldn't wait to get me into his book. I somehow managed to keep my mouth shut when he cautioned me, but I had to produce my documents, as I was driving a car that belonged to a friend of my mum's – my own car was in the garage for repairs at the time. Unfortunately, when I came to produce the

documents, it turned out that I'd been given a forged test certificate – I'd had no idea. I was presented with a '164 form', for the
speeding offence and for not having a valid test certificate, and I
received a fine of ten shillings. I expect some of my haters might
have hoped I'd be kicked out of the police force for that, but I
took responsibility for my actions and pleaded guilty to the
offence. I'd learned the lesson that as a driver, you should always
make sure your car's papers are in order.

I vividly remember another complaint made about me. This
one was from a police officer who I encountered one afternoon
when he was out in Leicester Square, with his wife and another
couple. I was walking up Cranbourne Street towards the nick,
where I was planning to write up my reports. Walking towards
me was the aforementioned bloke who, as I would later find
out, was a uniform sergeant who worked at a nearby station.

Being six foot one and pretty strong, I was able to stand my
ground when patrolling the streets – though I'd always move out
of the way for ladies or the elderly. On this occasion, the pave-
ments were wide, but I noticed this bloke whisper something to
his mate before heading straight for me. If he thought I'd get out
of his way, he was mistaken – I held my ground and we bumped
into each other. The force of my rock hard right shoulder
knocked him off balance slightly, but I thought no more of it.
The next time I saw him was at Bow Street Police Station, when
he complained to the sergeant that I'd deliberately pushed myself
into him. How childish! I was pretty sure he'd been the worse
for wear at the time – he was lucky I hadn't arrested him for
being drunk and disorderly. I was made to apologise, even
though it was obvious that I'd been the victim of a set-up.
Anyway, I hope he felt proud of himself!

One night, I arrested an old lag for stealing a sack of potatoes
from Covent Garden market. When he attended court the next

morning, he was in an aggressive mood. 'Us criminals have no chance,' he complained from the dock. 'I couldn't see the Black officer in the dark.' There were roars of laughter from the gallery and the magistrate had to quieten the court. Before sentencing him to three months, he smiled at me and remarked, 'I should think that is quite an advantage, would you say, PC Roberts?'

Other interactions in court related to my growing notoriety on the streets of Central London. A defence barrister once asked me whether I had a nickname. I didn't know what to say, but when the judge pressed me for a response, I shrugged my shoulders and said, 'The Copper with the Chopper'. The court had to be adjourned for a few minutes as everyone was in stitches, especially my fellow officers, who'd guessed what I was going to say.

Then there was the time that a defence barrister got me mixed up with one of the few other Black officers who had by this point followed my lead and joined the Met. While at the Crown Court one day during the trial of a prolific burglar, the defence barrister told the court that my nickname was Jacko, which I naturally denied. I didn't know Michael Jackman, who was a cadet stationed at Harrow Road, but it seemed clear that I was being confused with him – either the barrister or the defendant obviously couldn't tell the difference between one Black man and another! This gives an idea of the times that I was living in and the racism that I had to confront every day.

The barrister didn't listen to me and insisted that my nickname was Jacko, to the point that the judge was forced to intervene. He asked me what my nickname was, and to howls of laughter from the public gallery and the packed courtroom – including the judge – I said, 'It's Nozzer the Cozzer, the High-Flying Rozzer.' Perhaps I should explain. To this day, lots of people shorten my name to Noz, and Cozzer and Rozzer are both slang terms for a policeman. I can't remember exactly who it was, but some wag had at some point given me that rhyming nickname, and it had stuck. After the laughter had subsided, the barrister sat down. There were no further questions from the defence; when the jury returned, having considered the evidence, the defendant was duly dispatched to be detained at Her Majesty's pleasure.

As the nicknames might suggest, even though many of the officers at Bow Street hated my guts and refused to have anything to do with me, I made a few good friends while I was there. One of them was Michael Whiting, a Welsh officer who tragically lost his life while attempting to stop a stolen car in Oxford Street. I'd often given him a lift home from the station, and I was one of a number of police officers who travelled by coach to his funeral in Wales. Another friend was Jonathan Jones, also a Welshman, with whom I continue to exchange Christmas cards to this day. Then there was Jim Craik, a Scotsman who lived near my mother in Bromley. Both Jim and his wife were good friends of mine, and we stayed in touch after he moved to Australia. Thinking about it now, I wonder if the fact that these men weren't local themselves explained why they were more accepting of me.

Although most of the other people I got on with kept their heads down around the bullies, fearing that they would be attacked themselves if they stuck up for me, one officer who dared to publicly take my side at Bow Street was David Stevens, a Canadian bloke who didn't seem to care that I was Black. I would later be best man at his wedding. He would often chat to me, only to find himself being picked on as a result. The same people who made my life a misery once arranged for his car to be towed away, and they also reported him for offences that would normally have been considered minor and dealt with by nothing more than a verbal warning.

I wish we could have supported each other more – we might have been a force for positive change, but the circumstances were such that whatever we might have done wouldn't have made any difference. He often got called a 'nigger lover' by other officers, and he eventually felt he had no choice but to resign, even before he'd finished his probation, an indication that if you did stand up to the bullies, you don't always win. Fortunately, I was made of sturdier stuff.

At times it was hard not to go along with the abuse, in order to feel accepted. I remember attending a party at the house of one of my colleagues and taking a doll as a present for his daughter. I'm ashamed to admit that it was a golliwog, which I realise now was not a wise choice! I thought that it would ingratiate me to him, as he was a good friend of the station bully.

I can see now that my decision to buy a toy that trivialised the racist abuse I was suffering at work every day was motivated by my desperation to be accepted. It was my way of coping with the pressure that I was under – after all, it was the sort of thing they'd buy, so I thought that buying it would make me feel like one of the gang. Of course, I wouldn't dream about doing such a thing normally, but I thought they'd laugh with me and think, *Oh, he can't be all that bad*. I realise now that it was a stupid thing to do; at the time, I just wanted to be liked. If we were all respectful and tolerant of each other, no one would find themselves in that situation.

I was trying to make fun of myself, in the hope that the bullies would like me. I realise now that it seems a bit pathetic, but critics of my behaviour would do well to think how they would behave if they were as lonely as I was in the late sixties. In any case, it didn't work – while my colleague appreciated the gift, he preferred the company of the bully!

The bloke who I bought the golliwog for emailed me not so long ago – he'd seen an interview in which I'd complained about the abuse I'd suffered in my early days in the Met. He criticised me for, in his words, 'running down the officers at Bow Street'. He was completely wrong, of course – I was just telling the truth, and the fact that he wasn't able to hear it was his problem, not mine.

Deep down, I expect this bloke is probably ashamed of how he behaved back then, but I know he'll never admit to it. He even wrote in his email that I had loads of friends at Bow Street, which shows just how deluded he is. How on earth could he know how it felt to be me? I can remember the feeling of the knives going into my back – hardly the behaviour of friends!

He's the type of person who will continue to insist he did nothing wrong in those days – he'll always dismiss his racist bullying as 'canteen culture'. He's stuck in the past, and it seems unlikely that he will ever change. We may think the situation is much better now, but people are still suffering in the way that I did in the late 1960s. As I write this, a report has just been published into the bullying of Azeem Rafiq, a British cricketer of Pakistani descent who played for Yorkshire between 2008 and 2018; he faced racist bullying from certain teammates on a near daily basis, but the name-calling was dismissed by many people as nothing but 'banter'. As always, some of the bullies seem to think they've done nothing wrong.

Let me say at this point that I've often heard it suggested that every new recruit was mistreated and that what I experienced was normal. The way I can explain it is that if you were Scottish, Irish or Welsh, you might be made fun of every now and then, but you would not be hated before you even opened your mouth, like I was – if you were white, you were at least given a chance. It is some comfort to think that in some ways, the abuse I received was nothing personal – the first Black policeman would have received the same treatment whoever they were, and I'm glad that I had the resilience to overcome it.

I'll also always be grateful to the members of the public who treated me with respect and made me feel welcome during those difficult times. It would be churlish not to also thank those colleagues who covertly tried to treat me fairly, but the truth is that many of them did not have the guts to stand out from the crowd and instead chose to lower their standards to be popular.

As far as they were concerned, it was preferable to be liked by a hundred coppers than to be friends with a Black copper and hated by a hundred others.

Just like the bloke who emailed me, many of my tormentors from those days are still in denial. They either try to forget their bullying or they try to minimise or dismiss it, but I'll always remember what it felt like. However, they have made me a stronger person, and I won't ever allow anyone to be treated the way I was. I've always tried to stand up for the underdog, and that's never going to change.

I recently received a request from John Rogers, an old colleague at Bow Street, for permission to include an anecdote about me in a book he was writing. The story is his to tell, but I thought the way he started the passage was quite telling:

> In my early days at Bow Street, I was always very conscious of the fact that I worked alongside very strong characters and it took a very brave individual to speak up or directly challenge inappropriate language or actions. Was that wrong, yes it was. Was I part of it, yes I was. Have I done anything to change it, yes I have. [. . .] I've read a great deal about Norwell over the years, and the shit and aggravation that he has endured. I modelled some of my career on Norwell, and I am a better man for knowing him.

I guess that sometimes it takes a while, but I thank him for having found the courage to speak out.

By the early 1970s there were two other Black officers in the force, but then one of them, Michael Ince, was killed when his panda car collided with an area car – an emergency response vehicle, fitted with blaring sirens – as they both rushed to the same call-out on Oxford Street in February 1971. He was just twenty-five. I'd never met him, and all I knew about him was that he was stationed at Holborn. The tragic accident was reported in the press, but I remember quite clearly first hearing about it when a disgusting police officer – the bully I've previously described – ran into the front office in Bow Street where I was working, jumping up and down while holding a newspaper report of the accident and shouting 'One down, two to go,' while looking me straight in the eye. His mates laughed and jeered raucously. Although I was used to having to put up with verbal abuse, hearing him say something so callous was a real shock. It made me feel sick, like I'd been punched in the guts.

Even faced with this provocation, I still felt unable to confront him, knowing I lacked the necessary support from my supervising officers to back me up. The phrase 'If you can't take a joke, you shouldn't have taken the job' kept going through my head, and I guess I believed it.

Looking back, the incident seems typical of the treatment I received at Bow Street. I didn't like it, but there was nothing I could do about it, so I had to take it on the chin. I guess there's a link to recent events and the Black Lives Matter movement – my life, the bullies were telling me, didn't matter. There was a disconnect between the message that was being sent down from the top – the Home Office was saying, 'we need more people like Norwell' – and the people who were already in the police force who had all these racist attitudes that made life for Black officers unbearable. Still, my shoulders were broad enough for others to stand on – I'm proud to have helped to prepare the path that others walked.

My first few years in the police force had been hellish, but I was gradually accepted. The barriers slowly broke down, as my colleagues realised that they didn't have any reason to avoid speaking to me. Gradually, they invited me to join their card games. To start off with, they would stitch me up and take my money, but I chose not to complain – it was just good to be included.

My participation in police sports teams also helped. I was increasingly thought of as just another policeman instead of 'the first Black policeman'; when my colleagues overcame their fear of an avalanche of Black policeman taking all their jobs and realised I was not a threat to them, they dropped their defences.

You may be wondering why I didn't quit the police force in these early days, in the face of victimisation, and I often ask myself the same question. Maybe it was plain pig-headedness, but every instance of adversity gave me the incentive to keep going. The more the bullies wanted me out, the more certain I was that I should stay. Also, I felt that I owed something to those men who had given me the chance to join the police force, and to the members of the public I came into contact with; in the face of my colleagues' hostility, their respect kept me going.

At first, the public must have found a Black policeman a fascinating novelty. I had to get used to being stared at, and people would seem relieved that I could reply in English and in an accent they understood. I remember a couple of old ladies tentatively approaching me while I was on duty outside the South African embassy. One of them planted her face about six inches from mine and said, 'Can you tell us the way to the post office?' I could tell that they were wondering if I understood them – and more importantly, if they would understand my reply. They need not have worried. 'Up there, love – second on the right,' I said, giving them a big smile. They both gave a start, and the other lady said to her friend, 'Cor blimey, he's one of us.' The first lady put her hand on my arm and said, 'Nice to meet you.'

By the end of my time at Bow Street, I'd made many friends in the area and received a warm welcome from the local community. All the harsh treatment I endured in the station was vindicated by something the Metropolitan Police Commissioner Sir Robert Mark said in 1972, while he was answering questions about an annual report:

I am on record as saying that I believe the person who has done more to promote good relations between the coloured communities and the police is PC Norwell Roberts. I think we have cause to be grateful to him and to the way he faced the strains and hostility from both sides.

I didn't really understand how what I was doing was so special – as far as I was concerned, I was only doing my job. However, the attention inevitably led to everyone in the media wanting to speak to me again, and Scotland Yard decided that I should take part in a press conference. Subsequently, there was a flood of articles in the national press, with headlines including 'Just an Extraordinary Copper', 'Norwell is Top of the Cops' and 'Praise to Norwell'. As many of the papers reported, I'd been at the dentist when I received the news of Sir Robert's praise – I was in the chair when they said, 'Oh, you're in the papers!'

I was at pains to point out to anyone who asked that all I wanted was to be a normal policeman, but I knew that was impossible. By this point, I was fed up with seeing my face in the press – I knew I was no more special than the other 250 police officers at Bow Street, and I hated being treated as if I was. It was time to become a bit less conspicuous by leaving my uniform behind.

14

Detective Roberts

I NATURALLY REMEMBER THE late sixties and early seventies from the perspective of a police officer, and I didn't see much of the age of 'free love' that people talk about now – for me, life didn't seem very different to how it had always been. Central London was a hard place, and most of the crimes that I encountered while I was working there involved drugs.

In those days, it felt like everybody you stopped was a junkie, especially in and around Covent Garden. I remember the first time I saw a drug addict. It was in the toilets at the market – he was injecting heroin, and had mixed it with water from the toilet bowl. His face was covered in sores and boils and he'd tied a dirty handkerchief around his arm and was trying to find a vein. It turned out that he was a registered drug addict who was getting methadone from a doctor; after he'd got his fix, he was a different person altogether.

Encountering people battling addiction and dealing with petty crime made me keen to get involved with bringing more serious criminals to justice. I left Bow Street in 1972 and continued my training at West End Central, where I began to work with a crime squad, part of CID. One of my first tasks at this station was pickpocket patrol in the West End. One day I was discreetly following a suspect whom I had seen attempting to steal from ladies' handbags. Unbeknown to me, one of the magistrates from Marlborough Street Court was walking nearby. Once I had sufficient evidence, I arrested the suspect for what we called 'sus handbags', which referred to a suspicious person who had attempted to steal property from handbags. At just that moment, the magistrate walked past, having seen everything, and said with a smile, 'No doubt you'll all be in my court tomorrow.' He was right – we were, and the offender was sentenced to three months in prison.

The courts system was harsh in those days, but it was effective – unlike now, when many criminals seem to regard a spell in prison as a badge of honour. In those days, you could receive a six-month sentence for a first offence; nowadays, you're more likely to receive a fine, a suspended sentence or parole. Back then, prison felt like a more effective punishment – once you'd done a spell inside, you wouldn't want to go back! Borstal would also knock younger miscreants into shape, preventing them from pursuing a life of crime.

Soon after my arrival at West End Central Police Station, I began to work in plain clothes and with members of the Flying Squad, an armed branch of the Serious and Organised Crime Command within the Met. They worked out of Scotland Yard and dealt with really serious crimes – mainly armed robberies. When they nicked people, they'd refer to it as 'taking people off the pavement'. The unit operated across London without adhering to divisional policing boundaries.

The senior detectives on the robbery squad there treated me with respect, which was a new and welcome experience. I was pleased when one of them asked me whether I would be interested in taking a permanent job with the CID. I'd never considered a long-term career in plain clothes, but I started to give the matter some thought.

At around the same time, I was approached to do my first undercover job. My task was to buy two ounces of heroin, which was worth about £2,000 – £2,500 in today's money. The moment that the gear was handed over, the officers supporting me would swoop. The bloke who asked me to help was from the Flying Squad – everyone looked up to him, and I was pleased to be getting recognition for my work. However, the job ended up going wrong, and it was my fault entirely.

I can remember what happened like it was yesterday. I got dressed up in my gear – a wig and dark glasses, jeans and a bomber jacket – and met an informant called John (not his real name, of course). The plan was that he would introduce me to the bloke who would sell me the heroin. The job was supposed to take place on Park Lane, near Hyde Park, where surveillance had been arranged to provide me with cover.

Unfortunately, when I got into the cab with John, the first thing he said was, 'He doesn't want to do the deal on Park Lane – he wants to do it in a house in Kilburn.' It was my first big test and I was faced with a split-second decision, but I had no idea what to do – should I go to Kilburn with him, or should I call off the job? I was out of my depth; I knew it was critical that the job was a success, so I said, 'OK, let's go to Kilburn.' But, of course, all the plans for my cover had assumed that I'd be around Hyde Park, and I hadn't realised they wouldn't be able to just follow me up the road. When the cab suddenly headed north, my backup were all thinking, *What the fuck's going on?*

As I would later learn, it's never advisable to conduct such operations in a place where there's not adequate cover. Of course, I realise now that my decision was totally stupid – I could have been ripped off, or worse. Anything could have happened.

So I went to the house in Kilburn, leaving behind the surveillance that was critical both for gathering evidence and for my security. I did the deal, handing over the money for the heroin, and returned to the police station at Notting Hill, feeling pleased with myself. But when I got there, expecting to be greeted with smiling faces, my contact from the Flying Squad asked me how I'd got on. I couldn't help but be a bit intimidated by him – he had a broken nose, and looked a bit like a villain himself.

'I've got it,' I said, smiling and showing him the bag of white powder.

'What the fuck's that?' he said.

'It's the gear!' I replied.

I thought I was the bollocks and was expecting a hero's welcome, but then he said, 'But where's the money?'

It then slowly began to dawn on me that something had gone wrong. I said, 'Well, the geezer's got it.'

'So where is he?' he said.

'I don't know – you've got him, haven't you?' I replied.

He pointed at the heroin and said, 'What the fuck am I going to do with that?'

'I don't know,' I said. 'I just did what I was asked.'

I had no clue. It would have made a good cartoon sketch, if it hadn't been such a serious business. At that point, the other Flying Squad officers all stood up. Their coats parted, revealing their guns. I thought they were going to shoot me for ballsing up my first job and losing two and a half grand of police money in the process. Luckily, there was a happy ending – the gangsters were arrested and the money was recovered – but it was pretty hairy for a while. It had been a steep learning curve and I'd been taught the importance of sticking to the plan. I'd certainly never make the same mistake again, and luckily I was cut some slack as it was my first job.

This was the beginning of my undercover career – something I try not to talk about too much, as I'm mindful of the need to protect myself and others. With this undercover work established as a sideline to my main job at West End Central, I decided to take up the invitation to apply for a permanent position within the CID – PC Roberts became Temporary Detective Constable Roberts. Being a 'TDC' would mean being sent back to uniform if I failed the exams or if it turned out that I was not cut out to be a detective.

★　　★　　★

While I was working at West End Central, I learned to be a 'thief taker' – a common phrase in the CID for someone who took the job seriously and was good at catching criminals. I enjoyed interviewing suspects, together with the new challenge of attending court more regularly. Once, my partner and I nicked a young Black lad under the much-maligned 'sus law', which allowed us to arrest people for suspiciously loitering in a public place with the intention of committing an arrestable offence. Although it was a useful tool in the fight against crime, some people complained that it was open to abuse and that Black youths were unfairly targeted – rather like 'stop and search' today. Its use would cause a riot at the Notting Hill Carnival in 1976; the police tried to arrest someone for pickpocketing, but loads of Black youths thought he'd been targeted because of his colour and started to throw stones and debris at the police, who responded with baton charges. Over a hundred officers and around sixty members of the public were injured.

On another occasion, I was on patrol on the corner of Regent Street and Savile Row, when the officer I was with spotted a pickpocket. When this lad was arrested, I was standing a few feet away and he did not notice that I was part of the operation. Despite the fact that he'd been caught red-handed, he continued to protest his innocence. When he uttered the cliché, 'The only reason you're arresting me is because I'm Black', my partner said, 'Don't be ridiculous – allow me to introduce my partner.' The suspect's face was a picture when he realised that his stock defence had been shot down.

Although I was glad to have left the bullies at Bow Street behind, every now and then I found myself having to deal with similar discriminatory attitudes. I was sitting at my desk at West End Central one day when a dinosaur of an inspector came into the office, saw me and said to one of the senior officers, 'Who's the Schwarzer?' By using the German term for a Black person, he was clearly hoping to have a laugh at my expense, but his joke backfired – one of the officers sharply told him that my name was DC Roberts and that I was attached to the murder squad. He walked out of the room with his tail between his legs; the message that his racist jibes were no longer welcome in the Met – or at least this part of it – had been received, loud and clear. It was the first time in my career that someone's outdated attitude had been confronted head on, and it made me feel wanted and part of a team. I was overjoyed at the thought that such racism would no longer be tolerated. There were more Black officers in the Met by this point, too – it felt like society was finally changing.

Such remarks were certainly becoming much less common. I was working with seasoned professionals; they did not approve of how I'd been treated at Bow Street and wanted to protect me. I was extremely happy at work, in stark contrast to my years as a PC. The only disagreement with my colleagues that I can remember was about jellied eels – the officers in the Flying Squad all loved them but I couldn't stand them, much to everyone's amusement.

As a TDC at West End Central, one of the most significant cases I worked on was one of the biggest robberies of the age, when £8 million was stolen from a branch of the Bank of America in Mayfair in April 1975. Most of the investigations were carried out by senior officers, but they would always take a TDC with them to take statements and help with the more menial side of police work. Eventually, seven men would be jailed for their part in the raid. The gang had an inside man, a bloke called Stuart Buckley who was working as an electrician in the bank. In court, he would admit that they had previously tried to drill through the vault's lock, without success. He eventually managed to obtain the combination to the vault by hiding in the roof space above it and peering through a hole in the ceiling as officials opened it. The alleged mastermind fled to

Morocco and was never seen again, while only £500,000 of what was taken was ever recovered.

As a budding detective, I was obliged to attend a CID course back at Hendon. There was then a ten-week course for TDCs, the first five weeks of which were spent learning about the Theft Act.

When I joined the police, we would arrest suspects under the Larceny Act of 1861, but in 1968 this had changed to become the Theft Act. As detectives, we needed to know all the acts and sections in great detail – our expertise would be relied upon when the 'helmets' (our nickname for uniform PCs) made an arrest. After interviewing the suspect, we would decide what they should be charged with and how the case should proceed. For instance, a PC might have arrested some-one for being drunk and disorderly but upon investigation it might transpire that they were wanted for more serious offences. He would then be handed over to the CID for further investigation.

There were blokes on the course from all over the country and we all got on really well. I remember suggesting to my new pals that we should go for what I called a 'Ruby Murray', the cockney rhyming slang for curry. They all looked completely bewildered, until I explained what I meant. A few days later, an Irish trainee who was in our group said, 'Do you fancy going for a Helen Shapiro?' Everyone looked confused until he said, 'You know – a curry.' When I corrected him, he said, 'I knew it was a singer – I just couldn't think which one . . .'

Away from the classroom, my course mates and I liked to play jokes on each other. One day, I brought in an empty specimen bottle and a bottle of beer. I went to the loo and poured the beer into the specimen bottle, before walking back into the bar. When no one was looking, I took it from underneath my jacket and started to drink it. All of my mates thought it was hilarious, but there were some staff there who would keep an eye on us and make sure we didn't misbehave. One of them reported me to the instructor, who asked me what on earth I was doing. When I explained that the specimen bottle contained beer, I was lucky that he saw the funny side of my prank; my accuser was left looking a little silly, and I was a hero to my new friends.

However, I soon got my comeuppance. One bloke who came from Somerset had brought some scrumpy with him, and he made a bet with me that I couldn't drink two glasses over lunch one day. We returned to the classroom at 1 p.m. I only had to last until 2.30 p.m., when the lesson would be over, but with about fifteen minutes to go I had to rush to the toilet, where I was as sick as a dog. Even though I'd lost the bet, the camaraderie in our group was strong and I was accepted by everyone.

At the end of the course I was asked to make a presentation, and I took the opportunity to tell the story of my police career in a humorous way – telling jokes about what I'd gone through was my way of trying to be accepted. The presentation ended with me reading out the following poem:

Here's the tale of a Black boy – a cheeky bastard, of course,
Who stepped out of line and joined the police force,
When the fuzz heard of that, they went quite pale with fright,
'Black Power' had arrived, 'and we're whiter than white'.
'He'll put a curse on us all, that black-faced sinner,
'And worse than that – he may eat us for dinner!'
'He'll practise voodoo and play the drums all day.'
'Let's just ignore him – he may go away.'
So they gave him the boot – kicked his arse every week,
But that saucy young sod turned the other black cheek,
Until Old Bill got wise and said, 'Be happy Noz.'
(When he smiled at night, they knew where he was.)

So he stopped sticking pins in effigies he made,
And now the honkies are mates with TDC Spade,
They'll buy him a drink and treat him to luncheon,
But they still look twice when he takes out his truncheon!

Some people might read this and think I was making light of
the abuse that I'd suffered at Bow Street, but that's not the way
I saw it. It was my way of making people question their opinions
and how they'd treated me, at a time when I was still afraid to
talk about how upset I'd been. I was pleased to tell my story in
a humorous way without lecturing my audience or ramming my
problems down their throats – and I think it worked.

At the end of the course, several of us put on a little concert
for our instructors in which we performed sketches that made
fun of their idiosyncrasies. During my sketch, I played the part
of an exaggeratedly bad ventriloquist. The act went down a
treat, even with the instructors who were the butt of our jokes.
I would bet that at that point, anyone in my class would have
fought my corner – I'd gained their respect.

15

Station to Station

HAVING COMPLETED THE course, I was a fully fledged detective constable and was transferred to Vine Street Station. It was 1974, and I was still only in my late twenties.

I should at this point explain that when it came to transfers, you didn't have any say in the matter – it was expected that you'd be happy to go wherever you were posted. Officers were moved around every couple of years; it was never explained explicitly, but the idea was that this prevented corruption – if an officer stayed at a station for too long, they could get to know the area's villains to the extent that they could be susceptible to influence. The problem with this arrangement was that you'd regularly find yourself at a new station, having to get to know the area – and its criminals – from scratch.

One night, while I was on duty at Vine Street, myself and a couple of other CID officers found ourselves dealing with a rather difficult prisoner – he was stroppy and uncooperative, refusing to answer questions. He was eventually charged with some sort of offence and was remanded in custody to appear at the Old Bailey. That was the last we expected to hear of him, but when he appeared in court he made an allegation about the treatment he'd received while in custody.

As the guy was unable to identify a single one of the officers he was complaining about, those of us who had been on duty that night were summoned to the Old Bailey and asked to stand in a line, so he could pick out the officers who had treated him badly. There were twelve of us – nine uniformed policemen and three of us in plain clothes – and surprise surprise, being the only Black bloke in the line-up, I was the only officer he could identify. It was obviously not the correct way to conduct an ID parade – I had no chance! You'd have thought he might have thought to mention that one of his abusers was Black at an earlier point – he obviously thought I was an easy target and decided to try it on, but the judge wasn't convinced; the bloke's allegations were thrown out and he was found guilty. I remember the judge smiling as he thanked us for taking part in the charade, which the defendant had manufactured in an attempt to deflect attention from his crime.

Having passed my sergeant's examination in 1976, I was posted to West Hampstead station as part of a system known as 'interchange', which had been introduced to ensure that police officers gained experience both as detectives and as uniform sergeants. The idea was that you would return to uniform for a year, after which you could go back to the CID as a detective sergeant if you wished. However, much of a detective's work relies on the cultivation of informants and the downside of all this moving around was that you would have to start afresh at each new station, having lost all the contacts you had previously made.

I hope it's not big-headed to say that I looked very smart in my new uniform, which had three stripes on the sleeves to denote that I was now Police Sergeant 27E – I'm sad now that I don't have any photographs of me wearing it. The first obstacle I had to overcome at West Hampstead was a relatively minor one; I found that there were several policemen there who shared my surname – a Cadet Roberts, a PC Roberts at Hampstead and a DI Roberts. However, as the only Black Roberts, I was the easiest one to identify . . .

This was my first supervisory role, and I embraced the responsibility. Together with three other sergeants, I found myself in charge of a relief that consisted of thirty-five police constables. One of the uniform sergeants who showed me the ropes was a bloke called Jonathan Nicholls. We got on well, sharing a sense of humour, and have remained friends to this day.

I'd been told during a sergeants' familiarisation course at Hendon that, as supervising officers, we should try to avoid associating with police constables, but I chose to ignore this advice. After all, I could vividly remember the rough time I'd had as a police constable at Bow Street, and I wanted the officers under my supervision to be supported in a way that I hadn't been. I resolved to ensure that all my constables were treated fairly – I would admonish them when their work was below the required standard, but when they did something that deserved praise I would make sure I congratulated them.

I found myself in a situation where I was supervising constables who were much older and more experienced than me – I'd not long turned thirty, while some of them had twenty years' service and were approaching retirement. However, even these older blokes treated me with the utmost respect. I soon got used to being called 'Sarge' – what a difference from my time at Bow Street! It's all changed since then, but in those days, the use of first names was discouraged. A PC would never call his reporting sergeant by their first name, and nor would a sergeant refer to an inspector in such an informal way.

My new responsibility required me to report on probationers, which reminded me of the days when I'd been unfairly assessed by my superiors – I was determined to be fair in all my reports. Of course, as a young sergeant, I was also reported upon myself, by an inspector who supervised me and offered advice. I'm happy to say that, unlike my past experiences, these reports were a fair reflection of my efforts – which was all I'd ever wanted.

There was a lot to learn about my new role, including how to complete process and breathalyser reports. As the station officer, I was in charge of the station during the night as well as during the day, which was quite a challenge. But the fact that I'd worked in the CID in the West End meant that I had a lot of experience to bring to the table, and was able to cope with whatever was thrown at me – I quickly began to warm to this supervisor business!

While I was at West Hampstead, I was privileged to be put in charge of the first beat crimes squad. It was commonly referred to as 'minor crimes', but I've always thought this name was rather misleading. Just imagine that you're an elderly lady who has had something stolen that is of great sentimental value but not worth much in monetary terms; you'd think the crime you had suffered was just as deserving of police attention as any other.

In my opinion, there's no such thing as a 'minor crime', and the desperate people I encountered were testament to this. I remember having to urgently dash from my post as station officer one night in order to take charge of a situation where a severely mentally ill man was threatening to kill himself. When we tried to confront him, he walked backwards, away from us, while slashing his arms with a razor blade. The man ignored our demands to put the blade down, so I decided to take charge of the situation. I had to make a snap decision, so I turned to my fellow officers. 'If we don't nick him here, we're going to end up chasing him all the way to Piccadilly,' I said. I rushed at him, causing him to drop the razor and comply.

With the situation resolved, we returned to the station and I completed the various reports that had to be filled out. The man was subsequently admitted to a psychiatric hospital. My actions had shown my ability to lead from the front, which gained me the respect of my officers, but the power didn't go to my head – all I wanted was to be someone who my junior colleagues could turn to for advice and support.

I enjoyed the responsibility of being in charge of the beat crimes squad and felt like I had something to prove – most of all, I was keen to impress the chief superintendent who had given me a chance. We would all socialise together, and it was one of the most enjoyable spells in my career. Some people might think of such 'team building' sessions as little more than an excuse to go out boozing, but they would only occur once all our work was finished and when we had some arrests to show for our efforts. I encouraged my team to work hard, but I thought it was important that we played hard, too.

Once, during a quiet night shift, I decided to have a bit of a laugh and painted two stripes of Tippex on either side of my face – the idea was that it would resemble the war paint of a Native American, just like in the films I'd loved so much as a boy. I then sat down and waited for a member of the public to come into the station, insisting that I would deal with them when they did.

I didn't have long to wait – after a few minutes, an old lady came into the station and asked for some directions. Keeping a straight face, I answered her question and she looked straight at me without flinching. I repeated myself to ensure that she got a good look at me, but to my surprise it had absolutely no effect – she behaved as if seeing a uniformed police sergeant wearing war paint was completely normal, much to my colleagues' amusement!

I can also remember being on duty when someone wearing a suit waltzed past me, having entered the station via the back door. I had no idea who he was and was a bit put out that he had not introduced himself as he ought to have done. When I challenged him, he told me his name; I would later learn that he was a high-ranking officer from Scotland Yard. When I asked him for some form of identification, he showed me his silver token, a sign that he was indeed a very senior officer. To be fair to the bloke, he later asked my supervising inspector at the station to congratulate me on the way in which I'd dealt with him. I had been polite and careful to address him as 'sir', just as I had been taught to do at training school.

I threw myself into my work as a uniform supervisor and was always prepared to get my hands dirty. I led from the front – I wasn't afraid to delegate, but I'd never ask an officer to do something that I wouldn't do myself. When we were dispatched to demonstrations, for instance, I would be out there with my PCs, rather than barking orders from behind a desk.

I was keen that the station should be a welcoming environment for new recruits, and practical jokes were a big way in which they were made to feel part of the gang. We'd send new recruits to the local pond and ask them to measure the depth of the water. Those of us who were not on another job would be observing from a safe distance, trying hard not to be heard laughing.

There was also a cemetery near the station and we'd occasionally send new recruits there, telling them that we'd received a tip-off that suspects had been spotted there. The officer would follow the path until they were right in the middle of the cemetery, only for a colleague who was in on the joke to jump out from behind a gravestone, causing him to soil his pants while fleeing at breakneck speed. Such moments helped to pass the time during night shifts, but there was never any hint of bullying. I was keen that the atmosphere was friendly and inclusive – having experienced bullying at Bow Street, it was important to me that everyone was in on the joke. The officer would always see the funny side of the prank, and he knew that one day he would be able to play the same trick on another unfortunate colleague.

In 1977, having served my year-long stint on interchange, my boss came to me and told me that he had both good and bad news. The good news was that I would be returning to CID as a detective sergeant. The bad news was that I wasn't moving anywhere – I'd be working upstairs at the same station – but I did not mind that one bit. I was only in my early thirties but had transferred between stations several times, so it was a relief to stay in a place where I was happy.

While I was stationed at West Hampstead, I sometimes had to visit Hampstead Police Station, the main office from where the top brass operated. The station had the curious address of 26 ½ Rosslyn Hill, NW3. When I first went there it was to see the chief superintendent, Richard Wells, who for some reason chose to conduct interviews sitting next to you rather than on the other side of a desk. While this was intended to make junior officers feel relaxed, it could also be quite disconcerting. Young, inexperienced policemen would often fall into the trap of saying more than they had intended!

The chief superintendent was a thoroughly decent man. I often played squash with him, though I never made the mistake of calling him by his first name when I did – he was always 'sir' or 'guv' or 'guv'nor', the latter two terms being used by plain-clothes officers when addressing their superiors. We would be summoned to see him at the station if we were in trouble, a bit like having to go to the headmaster's office to receive 'six of the best'.

While I was at Hampstead there was a magistrate there called Mr Strachan, who always seemed to find a reason to give crimi-nals a second chance. The criminals thought of him as a soft touch and all hoped he would be the one sentencing them, but he changed dramatically when his own house was burgled. After that, every criminal who appeared before him found themselves sentenced to six months in prison, the maximum a magistrates' court was permitted to give and typical of the harsh sentences of the day. If the case warranted it, he would also remand criminals to the crown court, where they could be given an even harsher sentence. It was clear that his approach to criminality had been fundamentally changed by being a victim, just as many people's views are based on their own experiences. It was all very well to be an idealist about justice, but Mr Strachan's views hadn't survived an encounter with the real world!

16

Back to the West End

I<small>T IS OFTEN</small> claimed that every police station is located within spitting distance of a pub, and Albany Street Station was no exception – the nearest pub was just across the yard from the nick! I moved there in 1978, remaining within the CID.

My new patch also included Tottenham Court Road Police Station, which despite being a stone's throw from where I'd started out, was very different in terms of its clientele. A far cry from what we called the 'junkies and tramps' that I'd kept control over while I was at Bow Street – one of the first crimes I investigated was the burglary of a furrier on Tottenham Court Road, with a number of fur coats stolen that were worth more than £100,000. Thankfully, most of them were quickly recovered, and a few collars were felt in the process – with those responsible receiving their just deserts at the crown court. The owner of the business was thrilled with how quickly we'd managed to track down the stolen furs and offered us coats at a fraction of the usual price as a gesture of his appreciation.

The camaraderie at Albany Street was good, and the station patrolled an area where crime was high, which made it a busy place to work. While I was there, I was an authorised shot, which meant I was qualified to use a firearm. However, I soon realised that should anything go wrong, senior officers would often bend over backwards to appease a criminal rather than support their officer. I wasn't alone in thinking this – during my career, I spoke to plenty of colleagues who felt disillusioned

I AM NORWELL ROBERTS

with the support they received from their superiors. There was a feeling that the lowly officers could be thrown to the wolves whenever it was politically convenient, and this led me to relinquish my license – it wasn't worth the trouble that could result.

The incident that made me change my mind began with an early morning search for a violent criminal. One of my colleagues told me that he had 'more form than Arkle', referring to the famous racehorse – his rap sheet was about two feet long, with convictions for crimes that included the possession of firearms. He was clearly very dangerous indeed.

Given the 'danger to life', we were armed when we went to arrest this thug, but when we got to his house, his sister told us that he wasn't there. We knew she was lying, as our intelligence had established that he had been at home all night. We identified ourselves as armed officers, produced an arrest warrant and told this woman that we knew that her brother was at home. In response, she became hysterical, waking up her entire household in the process.

When we entered the premises, we were greeted by a barrage of abuse. The family were Black, so the decision was taken that I should lead from the front. The suspect's mother, despite knowing full well that her son was a dangerous criminal who was wanted for numerous offences, started shouting at me, telling me that I was a disgrace – she seemed to think that because I was Black, I should have been on her family's side instead of going over to the 'other side' and joining the police force. I had no time for this argument – as she well knew, I was only doing my job.

A search of the property revealed that her son was hiding in the attic; he was duly arrested, but the family continued to kick up a stink. They made an official complaint, accusing me and other officers of causing them distress by threatening the family and turning up armed. Of course, it was a pretty transparent attempt to deflect any blame from the suspect, and it did not work; he went to court and was found guilty, receiving a lengthy prison sentence.

I had absolutely no regrets about my behaviour and would have acted in exactly the same way if I was faced with the same situation again, but I couldn't help but feel that the investigation was more sympathetic to the criminal than to the policemen who'd risked their lives arresting him. I felt let down by the system and decided to relinquish my authority to carry arms. The offender's family didn't like the police, and they certainly didn't like the fact that their son had been arrested by a Black officer. The system paid more attention to their complaints than it should have, so keen were the powers that be to keep the public happy. It seemed obvious that the complaints system needed to be revised – I couldn't believe that an officer who had been doing their duty under difficult circumstances could be rebuked, just to appease the family of a criminal when they had the gall to complain.

Although I can foresee a time when police officers are armed as a matter of course, I'm pleased that the routine arming of police in this country is still some way off. It sometimes seems that the public yearn for a return to the sort of community policing seen in the classic TV series *Dixon of Dock Green*; a time when common sense and human understanding were more frequently deployed than firearms. In those days, of course, the police didn't have access to CCTV and the many other techno-logical advantages that they have nowadays – they were reliant on help from the public. Life was also, in reality, very different from our nostalgic, rose-tinted view, but criminality has got more brutal since then, and the hi-tech modern police force has developed in order to protect us.

In 1979, my CID office moved from Albany Street to Kentish Town in North London. There was no shortage of crime in this area – it was pretty rough, and a lot of people in the neighbour-hood seemed to fancy themselves as gangsters. However, while these thugs may have been regarded as tough in their commu-nity, it was a different matter when they came up against a police officer who was willing to confront them head on.

Haverstock Comprehensive School, where I'd attended as a pupil, was on my new patch – it was strange to think that my life had come full circle. In fact, I found myself attending the school to investigate a burglary and met some of the staff, who seemed proud to learn how my life had progressed. 'Maybe you did pay attention in class after all!' one of them joked.

Soon after I'd started working in the area, one young man verbally attacked me during questioning. Seizing the oppor-tunity to show him that I was no pushover, I decided to give as good as I got. 'You think you're hard, don't you?' I said. 'So do you,' he replied, to which I responded, as quick as a flash, 'Yeah, but I'm nice with it.' At this, something seemed to change in him. His frosty exterior thawed, and from that moment he was putty in my hands.

On another occasion I attended a burglary. As usual, I produced my warrant card at the front door of the victim, a woman in her eighties, but she didn't even look at it and just ushered me into her living room. 'Aren't you going to check who I am?' I asked. 'There's no need – you look like a policeman,' she replied. Given that I was six foot one and Black, and was wearing plain clothes with a kipper tie and a silk handkerchief in my top pocket, I was more than a little surprised at her remark!

A particularly embarrassing incident occurred when I was on night duty and one of my colleagues came into the office on his way home from a night out. We spent an hour or so putting the world to rights, during which time he discarded a cigar he'd been smoking in a bin without stubbing it out properly. It was only after he'd returned to his digs in the section house next door to the station that I noticed that the bin was alight.

I tried to put out the fire to no avail, so I ended up putting the bin on a flat roof outside the office and dousing it with water. It was an idiotic thing to do – the roof was made of asphalt, and it started to burn slowly. I poured more water on it, only for it to trickle through the damaged roof into an office below.

By this point I was panicking. I had to do something – but what? In my desperation, I decided to invent a story about an intruder climbing onto the roof and causing the damage. No one else was around, so I wrote this up in the night duty occurrence book before heading home at the end of my shift. Suffice to say, my ridiculous story did not convince anyone and I was summoned to the station the next day, where I admitted the truth. However, I chose not to snitch on my colleague who had started the fire – that wasn't my way. I just accepted my bollocking and moved on.

From my experience of living in Bromley as a boy, I'd assumed that people outside of London would generally retain the small-minded, racist attitudes that I'd encountered in suburban Kent. During my time at Kentish Town, I was required to travel up to Saltcoats, a small town on the west coast of Scotland, to collect a suspect and bring him back to London. When I arrived at the small police station, I greeted the detective at the front desk. 'I bet you didn't know I was Black, did you?' I said. 'So what if you are?' he replied. I was a little taken aback – in those days, a Black policeman was still a rare sight in London, and I couldn't imagine there were many Black people in this part of rural Scotland, let alone Black policemen! The fact that he didn't bat an eyelid was refreshing – I'd been accepted at face value, which was still a novel experience after a lifetime of judgemental attitudes. I suppose by this time racism was such a common occurrence in my life that I'd come to expect it.

I had a similar experience a couple of years later, when I was required to fly across to Ireland to pick up a prisoner who had been arrested for committing an armed robbery. Just as in Saltcoats, I was surprised to find that the officers there did not seem at all bothered about my colour. I was treated very well by everyone I met, and the bonus was that I was able to bring back some duty free. I remember the prisoner I was chaperoning looking thrilled when I gave him a bottle of whiskey to carry through customs; his smile soon disappeared when I took it back from him once we were through, thanking him for carrying it for me!

17

Moving up the Ladder

IN 1981, THE time came for me to leave Kentish Town. Having established myself at a police station, I was sad to have to relocate once again – this time to Acton in West London. On my first weekend there, I was greeted by a couple of experienced officers. 'Morning, Sarge,' they said, 'have we got a tough one for you.' They went on to tell me that during their night shift, a couple of prolific criminals had been caught red-handed during a burglary. They had been arrested and brought back to the station, but – hardened criminals that they were – they were refusing to speak. I was not alarmed, having had plenty of dealings with suspects who had exercised their right to silence, but I knew that such situations required careful handling.

Later that morning, I went and introduced myself to the burglars. Of the two, one of them clearly thought of himself as a bit of a hard nut. The first thing he said to me was, 'I want bail, I want to see my wife and I want something to eat – in that order.' I didn't care how aggressively he made such demands – there was no way he was going scare me into treating him differently from anyone else. He then started spouting the names of a few high-ranking officers who worked on other units in the area, in a rather threatening way – I think he was attempting to frighten me into letting him get his own way by suggesting that he had connections with senior officers. However, I was not in the least bit scared and just carried on with my enquiries – if this thug thought he'd be allowed to call the shots, he had no idea who he was dealing with.

It was at this point that I noticed that this menacing suspect had a large scar on the side of this face. It went all the way from his ear to the corner of his mouth – it looked like he'd been slashed with a knife, a clear sign that he'd upset someone dangerous at some point in his criminal career. 'I've no idea how you can think you're so hard,' I said. 'Surely the real hard nut is the person who striped and decorated your boat?' I'd been deliberate in my use of the shortened version of the cockney rhyming slang 'boat race', meaning face – I wanted to show him that I'd been around the block a few times and knew how to give as good as I got.

Once he realised that he couldn't mess me around, not only did he cooperate with our investigation, but we actually got on. It was another example of how knowing how to communicate with criminals was a big help – I guess my experience of dealing with the criminal community at Kentish Town came in useful, as I was not in the least bit frightened by him and his gang. He was charged with robbery and ended up on trial at the Old Bailey, where the judge told him that he should expect to spend the next few years at Her Majesty's pleasure.

My superiors at Acton were aware of what I'd achieved at West Hampstead and I was put in charge of a successful beat crime squad. As a detective sergeant, I had a level of seniority but was still among the boys on the shop floor. I didn't have any desire to be promoted any further up the chain – the politics of police work didn't interest me, and nor did the endless meetings that senior officers had no choice but to attend. Instead, I was happy working alongside a good team of officers. We worked hard, and the local villains respected us.

After we'd been working together for a while, a few of us started to call ourselves 'the A-Team', a reference to the American TV series that was very popular at the time. I was the captain, and the two detective constables who worked with me, Keiron Cotter and Chris Armstrong, were my lieutenant and sub-lieutenant. It was just a bit of fun, but there was some truth to it – we were good thief takers and always seemed to be at the top of the tree when it came to the number of arrests we made. In fact, we were so effective that the name gradually began to stick, including with some of the criminals. I thought of myself as Mr T, of course – the big Black leader of the gang. We looked and acted the part – whenever we arrested anyone, we would say, 'You've just been nicked by the A-Team.'

It was at around this time that a British cop show called *Wolcott* was launched, with a Black detective as the protagonist. Black police officers had been seen in television dramas before, but they'd always been American. George William Harris starred as the maverick detective Winston Churchill Wolcott, and I watched the show with interest, fascinated to see how the show would portray the character, given the similarities to my own life and career. Wolcott had come to England from the West Indies as a boy, just like me, and he also received a frosty reaction from his colleagues in the police force. However, even allowing for dramatic licence, the show seemed far-fetched, portraying policemen as doing very little police work and instead spending all their time running around, all guns blazing.

I have no idea if the programme's creators had considered getting in touch with me, but I remember thinking that they could have benefited from my insight. After all, the series was supposed to be about one of the first Black British detectives, so who would have been better placed to give a first-hand account? I enjoyed seeing the life of someone who looked like me on television, but I couldn't help but think that the producers of the series had missed an opportunity to promote the police force to the Black community; if it had been more accurate it would also have represented a way of educating the public. In the end, I decided to write them a letter, explaining that my experience would have given the show a degree of authenticity. However, I never received a reply, and the show was cancelled after a single series.

One incident when the colour of my skin did seem to cause confusion at Acton was after I'd spoken to the victim of a burglary over the phone and arranged to go and see her. When I arrived at her home, I introduced myself. 'Good afternoon,' I said, 'I'm Detective Sergeant Roberts and I've come about your burglary.' 'Yes,' she replied, 'I'm waiting for him.' She didn't realise that I was the police officer she'd spoken to, and I suppose the reason for her confusion was that she didn't think my accent matched my face. I didn't feel upset at her assumption – I could tell that she meant no harm. She spent the next five minutes apologising for the error, and we both saw the funny side of what had happened – I certainly didn't feel like I was being discriminated against.

Another encounter with an elderly lady was particularly poignant. She came into the CID office at the station to report a theft and during our conversation I noticed that she had a long number tattooed on each forearm. Being a bit nosy, I asked her what they meant – I'd never seen anything like them before, and my initial thought was that she'd written something on herself as a reminder. I was stunned when she told me that they'd been tattooed on her when she'd been in a concentration camp as a young woman, four decades earlier. She and her husband had been imprisoned together; she'd managed to make it out, but he had not. I was humbled by what she had gone through and found myself close to tears.

It was while I was working at Acton that I noticed a couple of my colleagues wearing Black suits and carrying little cases. When I asked them where they were going, they were tight-lipped. 'To a meeting,' they said. I was none the wiser, and I only realised some years later that that they'd been going to a Masonic meeting. In those days, membership of the Freemasons wasn't something that you advertised.

It was also at around this time that the brigadier who was in charge of a TA centre in Hammersmith where I'd been helping to train some 'wayward youths' asked me if I was a Freemason. When I told him that I was not, he asked if I'd be interested in joining. I asked what it entailed, and he was rather vague. 'Nothing,' he said. 'You just have a meeting with a few blokes, have a meal and then go home.' It was only once I'd joined that I discovered that there's quite a lot more to it than that. But being a member enabled me to meet a few like-minded blokes who shared a desire to support charities and other good causes.

Many allegations have been made over the years about the links between Freemasonry and the police; it has been said that criminals are not investigated if they are masons, or that judges give lighter sentences if they know the accused to be 'on the square'. While there's no doubt that both criminals and corrupt police officers have been Freemasons in the course of the organisation's long history, no respectable Freemason would dream of being involved in such dishonest activities. Too few people are aware of the many cases that have existed of members being arrested and sentenced by their fellow masons.

Although I didn't think being a Freemason was something to be ashamed of, it was, for some reason, a thing that many people did not publicly admit to. A few years later, I heard an officer singing a song that I recognised as something that was sung at the Masonic Festive Board. I looked him straight in the eye. 'You're a Mason,' I said. 'Not me – I wouldn't be one of those,' he quickly said. I couldn't help but smile – he'd always been quick to make fun of the masons, but he would later admit that he was in fact a member. Busted!

Freemasonry has been a big part of my life for a long time. It's an organisation in which I've always been made to feel accepted;

the warmth I've been shown is a far cry from the treatment I received in the dark days of my early police career. Furthermore, there are organisations for men and women in which all manner of people are represented – from a road sweeper to a stock-broker, everyone is made welcome.

One of the memorable cases I dealt with during my time at Acton involved an individual who would later go on to become rather notorious, but for tragic reasons. Errol Walker had committed a number of robberies all over West London, with his targets including post offices and betting shops. He would burst into a shop with an accomplice, brandishing a shotgun and wearing a black bomber jacket and a crash helmet with the visor down. Having seized as much cash as was held on the premises, the pair would make their getaway on a motorbike. One day, Walker robbed a post office in West Acton before fleeing to Greenford, where his accomplice was arrested shortly after-wards. Walker was on the run after the robbery, and decided to break into an old lady's house and hide in one of her bedroom cupboards, but he was soon discovered. I was involved in Walker's arrest, and afterwards I handed him over to the Flying Squad, who wanted to question him about other crimes he may have committed. I think they hoped to make him the first Black supergrass. I lost track of what happened to Walker at that point, and when I next heard of him, two years later, he was making headline news.

At just after 11 a.m. on Christmas Day in 1985, Walker climbed through an open window into the flat of a lady called Jackie Charles in Northolt, West London. Jackie was the sister of Walker's estranged wife Marlene; police were called to the scene when she staggered from the apartment block after being stabbed in the neck and thrown out of a third-floor window. She would later die of her injuries in hospital.

Before Jackie's tragic stabbing, Marlene had gone to the flat to see Walker; he had tried to drag her inside, but she managed to cling on to a railing and ran away. Walker then barricaded himself inside the flat, holding Jackie's four-year-old daughter at knifepoint and demanding he be allowed to speak to his wife. He held the girl hostage for the next twenty-nine hours, at one point dangling her out of the window and threatening to stab her. Next, he hung her over the edge of the balcony and smashed a police radio against her head, while firemen stood below with a safety net. He shouted at the police officers, 'I've done her mother. I'm not scared to drop her. It doesn't matter if I kill her because I've already killed – I'm going to do life anyway.'

Television cameras swarmed around the scene, with millions of viewers following events from their homes as they were happening. The siege finally ended when Walker dashed from the door to pick up a police shield that was lying on the balcony, before running back in. The police siezed this moment as their chance to get in without negotiating further and decided to storm the flat. They broke down the door and piled in after Walker, only to find him holding the girl in front of him, a knife to her throat. They shot him in the shoulder but he didn't drop the weapon, so they shot him in the temple at point blank range. The controversy in the wake of the incident was caused by the gap between the gunshots, which some saw as evidence that it was an attempted execution – far from the way in which we were trained to neutralise a threat. Remarkably, Walker some-how survived, though he would spend the rest of his life with a bullet lodged in his brain.

Meanwhile, the four-year-old girl was left with knife wounds to her neck and arms. The police faced a great deal of criticism from the local community and the press; many people suggested that they had overreacted, but they maintained that their response had been proportionate. As they said in a statement, 'From the outset, the intention was to prevent further injury.

But Walker was armed with a long-bladed kitchen knife and showed considerable instability and irrational behaviour. In the end, we had to storm in.'

At the height of the siege, I contacted the officer who was in charge of the operation and volunteered to go and talk to Walker. I explained that I'd dealt with him a few years earlier and suggested that he might find it easier to talk to me – not just because I was Black like him, but because I was a trained hostage negotiator and knew from experience that enlisting the help of someone who has a rapport with an aggressor can pacify a tense situation. However, on this occasion, my offer of assistance was declined.

Walker would later be convicted for the murder of Jackie Charles and jailed for life. As a side note, Tony Long, the police marksman who shot him, was involved in several more controversial shootings in his career; it would later emerge that some of his colleagues in the Met knew him as 'the serial killer'. In 2005, just months before he was due to retire, he shot and killed a young man called Azelle Rodney at point-blank range, following intelligence that he was a member of an armed gang that was about to steal drugs from some Colombian rivals. He was charged with Rodney's murder, but was eventually acquitted by a jury at the Old Bailey.

To this day, I'm sad that my offer of assistance wasn't taken up – with my involvement, I believe that the siege might have been ended peacefully. It felt like a running theme in my career – the police could have taken advantage of my presence and used me within the Black community, but they were always reluctant. I didn't necessarily want to act as a spy, but I had a rapport with the Black community and could have shown them that there was someone on the 'other side' that they could talk to. Taking advantage of that cultural understanding just seems like common sense to me. I mean, if there's something wrong with my car, I'll get a mechanic to look at it – I wouldn't ask a solicitor to help!

The Met were happy to use me as a poster boy when they wanted to show off about what they were doing – why did they not want me to engage with London's Black population directly?

After the fatal stabbing of the ten-year-old schoolboy Damilola Taylor in Peckham in November 2000, the Black police superintendent Leroy Logan was asked to lead a team of Black officers tasked with conducting house-to-house enquiries in that area of South London – the idea was that if they seemed like part of the community rather than the enemy, they might be able to overcome the 'wall of silence' that prevented people in the community from speaking out about what went on. The team, which would later be formalised as the Cultural Communities Resource Unit, did some crucial work that helped to identify Damilola's killer; essentially, they were doing what I'd suggested fifteen years earlier. All progress is positive, of course, but I still wonder why it took so long.

It was while I was at Acton that I received my first commendation for detective work. In 1985, I was the lead detective in a case that resulted in the arrest of five men for murder and conspiracy to commit murder, following the death of a young man. Initially, it seemed like a contract killing. It would turn out that an uncle had paid someone to murder his niece's boyfriend because the youth was too Westernised to be deemed an acceptable match. All he'd wanted to do was warn him off; unfortunately, the blow had been inflicted with such force that the victim crumpled to the pavement, dead before he hit the ground.

The culprits escaped in a car, but we were fortunate that an observer made a note of the registration plate and gave it to us. A search of the number took us to a tower block in Hackney. We had no idea of what flat number they lived in, so we staked them out, waiting outside the building and arresting the suspect when he left and went to his car.

We took him back to the station for questioning, but he refused to tell us his address. At that point, I decided to step things up a gear. 'You don't have to tell us your address,' I said, 'but surely you want us to phone your wife and let her know that you've been arrested?' That was all it took; he fell for my plan and gave us his phone number and once we had it, we were able to locate his flat and find evidence appertaining to the crime.

Our enquiries would take us to Coventry, where we arrested five men and charged them with conspiracy to commit murder. They appeared at the Old Bailey and were found guilty, receiving lengthy prison sentences. This was one of my most rewarding pieces of work as a detective, and it had only been possible thanks to the member of the public who supplied us with the registration plate – once we had that information, the rest was easy. Sometimes the real skill lies in developing a rapport with the public that allows you to enlist their cooperation.

During the trial, the barrister who was defending the criminal who gave me his phone number protested that his client had been tricked into supplying it. 'Well, of course I did!' I replied. In my opinion, this was no infringement of the bloke's rights – it was just skilful investigation. After all, it's the job of a CID officer to use all the legal methods available to him, including guile and cunning. That's just what we do.

During the course of the investigation, something happened that took me right back to my Bow Street days. I was with two Black officers and we'd just driven back to London from Coventry, having made the arrests. We were exhausted but pleased – the case had been brought to a successful conclusion, and we were excited about sharing the good news with our colleagues. As we walked into the packed meeting room, a hush descended and everyone turned to look at us. 'Here come the Schwarzers,' said a detective inspector, using the insult that I'd had to put up with earlier in my career. I may have been too scared to respond to such remarks when I was younger, but by this point I was a forty-year-old senior policeman with a great deal of experience; I flew into a rage at his use of the racist slur and had to be physically restrained from punching him. This time, the detective superintendent who was in charge of the operation backed me up. 'He's a real pillock and that was completely out of order,' he said. 'And if you'd punched him, I'm sure everyone would have looked the other way.' This was nice to hear, and much more supportive than the comments I'd had to put up with when I complained about racist abuse earlier in my career – things like 'What do you expect me to do about it?' The sad part, of course, was that the detective inspector faced no repercussions; racism still seemed to be an ingrained issue in the police force nearly twenty years after I signed up.

At most of the stations where I worked, there would be a weekly staff gathering every Friday at 5 p.m. All ranks would be encouraged to attend and we'd have a few drinks. Sometimes, uniformed officers would also attend and thank us for the week's work. At one such event during my time at Acton, it got to about 7 p.m. and there were just a few stragglers left. As the DS, I was in charge; there were four DCs still there, as well as one uniformed PC who'd had a few too many drinks. When he left, he was clearly the worse for wear. As he was leaving the station, his supervising inspector asked him where he'd been drinking. He told him that he'd been in the CID office.

This particular inspector had not attended the gathering, though he'd been aware that it was taking place. As a result, the PC was reported for being drunk on duty, and as the most senior CID officer on duty, I was hauled over the coals. It was ludicrous – as if I could have done anything to prevent an officer with twenty-five years' service getting into such a state! Whatever happened to people taking responsibility for their actions?

The result of all this was that I was transferred to Ealing CID for 'closer supervision', but the ridiculous thing was that everyone there knew why I'd been transferred. It also turned out that when I got there, Ruislip CID were short of a senior officer – one of them was working on a case that was being heard at the Old Bailey – so guess who was asked to go to Ruislip to be the acting detective chief inspector, two ranks above mine? So much for me needing to be under closer supervision – the whole thing made absolutely no sense. It felt like I was being set up to fail, but I just tried to do my job – exactly what I'd been doing throughout my career.

18

Back on the Beat

I FELT A SENSE of trepidation at the start of my secondment to
Ruislip in 1983, but I thankfully managed to make a success
of it. I was welcomed by the other officers, who respected me
and treated me like their DCI. Once my short spell there was
over, I was back in Ealing and once again in charge of a beat
crime squad. We worked in pairs and competed to outdo each
other, seeing which team could make the most arrests. The
element of competition could lead to friendly rivalry, especially if one pair overheard another discussing an operation
that was planned for the next day and resolved to get in there
first.

Together with a couple of DCs, I decided to form another
'A-Team', just as I'd done at Acton. Once again, I was Mr T,
while Colin Weekes and Andy Smith fitted the characters of
'Howling Mad' Murdock and Lieutenant Templeton Peck.

We were arresting a prolific burglar who had evaded arrest
for some time, when one of my team happened to joke, 'You've
just been arrested by the A-Team.' We thought no more of it,
but the suspect told his solicitor, who in turn passed on the
information to his barrister. When the case reached the crown
court, he recounted the story in an attempt to make us look
unprofessional. I was in the witness box and found myself being
berated by the defence barrister for referring to ourselves as the
A-Team. My mates from the squad who had already given
evidence were sitting in the public gallery and were desperately

trying not to laugh. The members of the jury also seemed amused, as they could see how we resembled the characters from the TV series!

Meanwhile, the judge didn't have a clue what the A-Team was – he was so perplexed that he had to ask the barrister to explain the reference. Once he'd been enlightened, he smiled and drolly said, 'Yes, I can understand the resemblance – I'll have to watch the series.' At this, the jury and those in the public gallery burst out laughing. Once order had been restored to the court, the jury retired, before returning a guilty verdict after just fifteen minutes. One of them later said that they would've been back within three minutes, but they'd had a cup of tea in the deliberation room to 'make it look decent'.

The judge sentenced the burglar to three years in prison, before adding that he hoped the A-Team would keep up their good work fighting crime on the streets of West London. All the jurors were keen to talk to us when the trial was over, with some of them even asking for our autographs.

During my time at Ealing, I was also asked to assist the CID at Southall Police Station, where they were investigating a local murder that was linked to recent events in India. There was a great deal of sensitivity in the Sikh community at that time; under the leadership of Jarnail Singh Bhindranwale, Sikh separatists has begun a campaign of terror to demand independence for the Punjab, and many of their opponents were murdered. In June 1984, Indian armed forces had stormed the Golden Temple in Amritsar where Bhindranwale had set up an armed occupation. Hundreds of civilians were killed, including Bhindranwale, heightening tension among Sikh communities all over the world.

In October 1984, Indira Gandhi, the Indian prime minister who had ordered the assault on the Golden Temple, was assassinated by one of her Sikh bodyguards. The following year, Sikh terrorism went international; militants planted a bomb on an

Air India flight from Montreal to London, causing it to disintegrate in mid-air while flying over the Atlantic Ocean.

This Southall murder enquiry gave me another insight into South Asian culture; the suspects were Sikhs, and I also found myself working with one of the first Sikh officers in the Met, who wore a turban instead of a helmet. He was also an interpreter and well known in the Sikh community, so he could generally tell if a suspect was lying to us. The public seemed to find it easier to talk to me when he was there to answer their questions. I'd never worked in an Asian community before, so it was a fascinating and useful experience.

After a couple of years in West London, I was transferred to Wembley, where I was put in charge of the crime desk, a role that I'd previously perfected at Acton and Ealing. It was not dissimilar to a mini CID, being comprised of uniform officers who were permitted to wear plain clothes.

The station's proximity to Wembley Stadium meant that I'd often be in charge of the ground's security, and this led to some interesting encounters when I was on duty at sporting fixtures or pop concerts. One of the most memorable was with Muhammad Ali. He'd come over to watch a fight – I think it might have been between James 'Bonecrusher' Smith and Frank Bruno in May 1984 – and I just went up to him. He said to me, 'Do I know you?' I said, 'No you don't – but can I have your autograph?'

Of all the cases I worked on during my time at Wembley, the one that I remember as being the most harrowing involved a man who had indecently assaulted a young lad. Just thinking about what this kid had gone through transported me back to my childhood and reminded me of how I'd felt after I was abused by my Uncle George. I was barely able to look at the perpetrator, but I somehow managed to grit my teeth and treat him fairly. I could tell that he thought I was going to give him a slap for committing such a heinous crime. I managed to restrain myself – though I can remember being pleased that he was scared of me, after the torment he'd put that poor child through.

I can also vividly remember a Black lady coming to the station in the early hours while I was on a night shift – her teenage son had been arrested for burglary and we were only allowed to question him in the presence of a parent or appropriate adult. She asked if she could speak to her son in private, but she ended up doing a bit more than that – when we rescued the lad, she was slapping him around in an attempt to teach him a lesson. She was West Indian and was chastising him in exactly the way that I'd been chastised back in Anguilla, which brought a smile to my face!

When I'd arrived at Wembley, I was told that I should avoid going to an area called the Chalkhill Estate on my own. A huge high-rise council estate of nearly two thousand flats linked by open walkways, it had been state-of-the-art when it was built in the late 1960s, but by this point it was a run-down crime hotspot. Robberies were so common that milkmen refused to deliver to people's front doors, and police officers had found themselves being pelted with bottles of urine from the balconies of the tower blocks. I listened to the warnings, but took no notice of them; I felt strongly that if police are to function properly, there cannot be such a thing as a 'no-go area' – that would mean giving in to the criminals. I decided to go to the estate alone, and I encouraged my colleagues to do the same; in this way, we were able to foster good relations with its residents.

One evening, we rushed to the estate having received a call that a man was standing on a first floor balcony and threatening to jump. We arrived to find that the fire brigade and an ambulance were already on scene. A police negotiator tried to reason with the man for two hours, and six uniformed officers were tasked with controlling the crowd. The man kept shouting down, 'I'm going to jump.' At one point, someone in the crowd shouted back, 'Well, go on then – bloody well jump, and then we can all go home.' Unfortunately, he did just that, breaking both legs in the process. It was lucky for us that it was not a police officer who had told him to jump – it would probably have led to a riot.

Working life at Wembley was a bit of a mixed bag. I enjoyed the work, but a couple of my colleagues tried to make things tricky for me. There was one particular senior officer who took a dislike to me because I used to get into work before him. He'd get to the station at about 6.30 a.m., hours ahead of my shift starting, but I used to arrive even earlier, and for some reason it really annoyed him. I have no idea why it used to upset him so much – it wasn't as if I was claiming overtime, it was just that I only needed three hours sleep each night. I'd be awake by 3 a.m. most days, and thought I might as well go to the station as I could get on with my work in peace without being distracted by constant phone calls. It is a practice that I've continued to this day – I'd rather be an hour early than one minute late.

This bloke angrily told me not to get in so early, but I took no notice. You can be sure of one thing – I was never late! I'd get there at 6 a.m., even if my shift didn't start until 9 a.m. The way I saw it, it gave me three extra hours every day to do a job I loved!

I was dedicated, which meant I wasn't always left in peace on my days off – but sometimes my specific input was required. I was off duty and relaxing at home one day when my phone rang. It was an officer from the station.

'Hello, DS Roberts,' he said. 'I've got a gentleman here for questioning, and he says he knows you.'

'Who is it?' I asked.

'A Mr Tony Moore,' came the answer.

I knew Tony well – he owned a wine bar in West Acton that I used to frequent with some colleagues from CID when I'd worked in that neck of the woods. I knew he was an honest bloke and guessed that there had been some sort of mistake, but I decided to play along. 'What's he done?' I asked. The detective explained that Tony had moved from Wembley and gone to live in Brussels, renting out his house to three elderly people.

However, these tenants had turned out to be well-known criminals who were carrying out a major credit card fraud. First, they would find an unsuspecting landlord – in this case they'd picked Tony, and the fact that he lived abroad made him an even better victim. They would then add themselves to the electoral role for the property and change the utility bills so they were in their names. After that, they would apply for a credit card and pay off a few small purchases in full, thereby increasing their credit limit. They would then repeat the process with as many credit cards as they could, before maxing out all the cards and doing a runner; with their tenants nowhere to be seen, the unfortunate landlord would end up being stiffed for his rent, as well as whatever they had taken from the house before they disappeared!

Even though Tony had travelled all the way from Brussels to assist with the police enquiry, the officers were not convinced of his innocence and grilled him for several hours about his relationship with his tenants, trying to determine whether he had known anything was dodgy. In a moment of panic, Tony had asked, 'Do you know Noz?' 'Noz who?' the detective asked, to which Tony replied, 'Nozzer the Cozzer – you know, Norwell Roberts?'

Fortunately for Tony, they knew who I was, and it was at this point that they called me up. Once I'd spoken in support of my old friend's character, the officers were convinced that he was telling the truth and chose not to take their enquiries any further. Tony *was* telling the truth, of course – the fact that he knew me simply helped to convince them of his innocence. I met up with him the following day and we had a good laugh about the matter over a couple of drinks.

★　　★　　★

During my police career, work took over my life to the extent that I didn't have time for much else, but one thing that I did enjoy was sport, from athletics and football to rugby and even tug of war. While I was at Wembley, I played cricket for the division, and we played our matches at the Metropolitan Police's sports grounds that were scattered around the outskirts of London. On one particular summer day in 1985, I was part of the team that went to the Met's sports club in Chigwell in Essex. I'd driven to the ground with a teammate who was mixed race and we were early, so went to wait in the bar, where we stood next to two elderly men.

The ex-policeman who was working behind the bar looked across at us and said loudly to one of the punters, 'I didn't think that they let that sort in here.' He was clearly alluding to the colour of our skin. I gave him an angry stare and we walked out without buying a drink.

I was fuming. This was nearly twenty years after I'd started at Bow Street, and I couldn't believe that we were still having to put up with that sort of casual abuse and idiotic, racist behaviour – and in a police sports club, of all places! My mate tried to calm me down, but the barman and the other customer kept staring at us and whispering among themselves, which made us feel uncomfortable. By this time, the rest of our team had joined us; when I told them what had happened, they couldn't believe it.

At some point, our abuser left the bar and was heading for the toilets, so I followed him with the intention of standing up to him and challenging his behaviour. However, when I got into the toilet, he was nowhere to be seen – he'd clearly ducked out the back exit to avoid trouble. That was probably just as well – if I'd found him, I'd have shoved him up against the wall and given him a piece of my mind, but I might well have got myself the sack in the process. We went on to win the cricket match that day, but it was little consolation.

As much as I tried, I just couldn't forget about the incident – it was a harsh reminder that not much had changed since the 'bad old days', which I'd hoped were far behind me. I hated the thought that the barman could laugh at people to their faces and get away with it, and I wanted to see him punished. In the end, I reported his behaviour to my chief superintendent at Wembley. I hoped that my complaint would be taken seriously, but it turned out to be a complete waste of time. He assured me that he'd speak to this equivalent at Chigwell about the matter, but I didn't hold out much hope that any action would be taken – I recalled what had happened at Bow Street many years earlier, when the senior officer promised to follow up my complaint about the racist policeman at Southwark but never did.

When I asked a few days later whether the barman had at least been spoken to, I was told in no uncertain terms that he'd denied the allegation and that would be the end of the matter. It was obvious that the incident had simply been swept under the carpet – yet again, a racist thug had abused someone and got away with it. I was hardened to such things by now, so rather than crying about it as I had at the start of my career, I just chalked it up as one more incident – another entry in the long list of slurs. The incident shows just how acceptable racist abuse was in the 1980s; British society may have been becoming more multicultural, but far-right groups such the National Front were an ever present on the fringes of politics and many people shared their vile views. The England football team may have had Black stars such as Viv Anderson and John Barnes, but they still had to suffer the routine indignation of fans taunting them with monkey chants or hurling banana skins onto the pitch.

I don't know why I expected the police hierarchy to take such racism seriously – after all, they had a long history of ignoring it. But still, I thought that after nearly twenty years' service, my complaint would have been investigated; instead, the powers that be took the easy option and did nothing, safe in the knowledge that I was too professional to create waves. Once again, by not admitting that there was a problem, they were able to avoid doing anything about it.

Every Christmas during my time at Wembley, a social gathering organised by the station gave people in the neighbourhood a chance to meet one another and the local police officers. It was through one of these gatherings that I became friendly with a local businessmen called Finlay Tinker, a kind man who owned the Dog & Duck pub, one of the oldest establishments in Wembley. Finlay would donate toys that I would give out as Father Christmas at a nursery for disadvantaged children, where my wife Wendy worked.

It's always been clear to me that the police are at risk of losing the respect of the public if we do not try hard enough keep them on our side. I made an effort to do everything I could for the community, which meant being on hand to help out in tricky situations. I remember being phoned up in the middle of the night by Michael, the manager of the Dog & Duck, who was worried about noises that seemed to be coming from the pub's cellar. He'd called me to ask my advice because I'd helped him out when there had been a bit of trouble at the pub. This time, I told him to ring the local police, but he was reluctant to do so – he didn't have much faith in them because he'd found them to be less than helpful in the past. He trusted me, so he asked if I'd come to the premises and investigate.

I quickly got dressed and drove to the pub, parking around the corner. Michael let me in through a side entrance and we tiptoed into the bar, from where we could see a hooded figure wearing a black balaclava standing next to the fruit machine. He was trying to prise it open with a large knife that the manager would later identify as having come from the pub kitchen. I picked up the nearest thing to hand – a bar stool – deciding that I had to do something, and fast. I gestured to Michael to get back before making my move. 'Drop the fucking knife and get on the floor before I wrap this bar stool around your head!' I shouted to the intruder, before letting out a couple more expletives and trying to be as menacing as possible.

It was fortunate for the thief that he did as he was told, as I'd have had no qualms about wrapping the stool around his head. I shouted at Michael to dial 999, and a squad car arrived a few minutes later and carted the criminal away. It later transpired that he was part of a gang who'd been breaking into pubs all over North London through the trap doors into the cellar that are located on the pavement outside.

Although it was a shame that Michael didn't have sufficient faith in the local police to contact them directly, the incident had a happy ending and demonstrated how the police and the public can work together to tackle crime.

While I was stationed at Wembley, I started spending a lot of my free time helping out at an attendance centre at Mill Hill. Such centres had been set up to offer an alternative form of punishment for young offenders and keep them out of prison; for many young men, the risk was that a prison sentence would inevitably lead to a life of crime from which they would be unable to escape.

The courts were empowered to order offenders to attend such centres when they were convicted of crimes that ranged from shoplifting and burglary to football hooliganism and assault. The centres were largely administered by the police; offenders were generally required to spend between twelve and thirty-six hours at the centre, which took the form of three-hour sessions every other Saturday afternoon. Failing to complete their hours would lead to a warrant being issued, and they would be taken back to court for an alternative punishment, possibly involving a custodial sentence. The timing of the sessions was deliberately planned as a deterrant; they lasted from 2 p.m. to 5 p.m., inconvenient for the offenders as they coincided with the time when they might normally be attending football matches.

The centre, which was based in a secondary school, was run by an inspector called Tony Harper and I was his deputy. The offenders came from all over Greater London, Hertfordshire and the surrounding counties. It was a way of giving wayward lads a purpose in life that didn't involve committing crimes on a daily basis.

I knew that if I could channel the lads towards a better life, I'd have put something back into society. I realised early on that discipline was key. I expected them to be there at 2 p.m. on the dot – even one minute past would be too late. It was the only way to teach them the importance of punctuality. If they were ever late, I told them they must apologise and explain why they hadn't been able to get there on time, and if they didn't have a good reason, I'd send them home and their attendance on that day wouldn't be counted – it was as simple as that. I reminded them that as a seasoned police officer, I'd been around the block and had heard all the excuses under the sun – if they were lying, I'd be able to tell.

Something about how they reacted gave me the impression that the thought of having to apologise was making them uncomfortable, so I quickly said, 'Don't worry – you don't have to mean it. But you *must* say it.' This seemed to work, and they were rarely late. On one particular occasion, one lad was twenty minutes late. He apologised and had an excuse that seemed convincing – I'd obviously got through to him.

The lads were of the age when they'd developed a resentment for authority, which meant that they'd occasionally try it on to see what they could get away with. They soon realised, however, that I had little tolerance for their games. One of the important things that I tried to instil in them was discipline – I wanted them to be able to go out into the big bad world and get a job. I also taught them the importance of respecting each other, and I started by showing them respect. I'd refer to them as 'Mr Smith' or 'Mr Jones', and I insisted that they call me 'Mr Roberts'. I wasn't stupid enough to think that they would be so polite in their everyday lives, though I naturally hoped that some of it would stick!

One particular lad seemed to be unable to stop himself from shoplifting – it was like he had an addiction. He'd been arrested seventy-eight times and received all sorts of sentences, from fines and conditional discharges to suspended sentences and probation orders. I remember pulling him aside one day, keen to get the bottom of what had drawn him to a life of crime. 'I don't understand what's going on in your head,' I said. 'Why do you do it?' What's the appeal?' He replied, completely serious, 'Well, Mr Roberts, it's just what I am. I'm a thief, in the same way that you're a policeman.' I was tempted to say that the difference between us was that while I was a good policeman, he seemed to be a lousy thief because he kept getting caught, but I managed to restrain myself.

We also set strict standards of hygiene. The lads had to turn up in clean work clothes, smoking was prohibited and the slightest hint of bad behaviour risked them having to go back to court. I organised sessions that encouraged the participants to consider the repercussions of their actions. We also covered subjects such as housing, how to claim unemployment benefit and first aid skills. Sometimes we arranged physical training sessions; in fact, one of the most difficult things about the whole job was convincing them to have a shower afterwards!

While I was at the centres, I'd arrange for local magistrates to come and to talk to the lads. Many of them sent me letters afterwards, complimenting me on the work I was doing. They were well aware that if the lads failed to attend a session, I could turn up at their homes and arrest them without any warning – they'd then be taken before the local court to be sentenced, sometimes by the very same magistrate who'd visited the centre. I think most of the lads would rather have paid a fine and kept their free time; despite this, I got some satisfaction from the idea that they were learning to be better people in their community.

In this period, I also used to visit a pub called the Chequered Flag. The pop star Gary Numan would occasionally drop in and play a few songs. Whenever he did, the pub's landlord would call me up and ask for my help, in case there was any crowd trouble – Gary was a global superstar at the time, so an impromptu concert in a suburban pub always caused a bit of a stir! I'd position myself near to the stage, to dissuade any undesirables who might have been tempted to get a bit too close.

After I'd helped out at a few of Gary's gigs, I got to know him quite well. He was trained as a pilot, and one Christmas he had a plan that would help make my Santa Claus duty at the nursery where Wendy worked a bit more exciting. He offered to take me up in his plane – the idea was that I'd be dressed up in my costume and he would pretend that he'd picked me up from the North Pole. All I had to do was to get the children from Wendy's nursery in Paddington to Blackbushe Airport, which I did by hiring a London bus. Wendy travelled in it with all the kids, and when they were about half a mile away from the airport, Gary took me up in his plane, a Cessna. I was sat in my costume when Gary said, 'Here – have a go,' and he handed me the controls. It must have been a very strange sight! Once we'd landed safely, the shock on the kids' faces was clear for all to see. Wendy and the other helpers said, 'Its Father Christmas – he's come all the way from the North Pole!' and I handed out all the toys.

On another occasion, the children were taken to see Father Christmas at Harrods. One of the three-year-olds said to him, 'You're not the real Father Christmas.' 'What makes you say that?' he asked. There was a sharp intake of breath from the nursery staff, who were nervous that the child might be about to say something about the colour of his skin – of course, this Harrod's Santa was white, unlike me. However, nothing could have been further from the little boy's mind; 'Because you don't come to our nursery,' he said. It seemed to me that the child could teach us grown-ups a thing or two about racism – rather than focusing on his skin colour, all he saw was a man with a big white beard dressed in a red suit and carrying a sack full of toys.

19

Working Undercover

THROUGHOUT ALL MY years in the Met, undercover work was a key part of my job – in the course of my career I was part of more operations than I could count. It meant a hell of a lot of risk – even if the criminal I was dealing with wouldn't have killed me if they found me out, they were never going to be very happy about it.

I remember being on a job once somewhere in the East End with the aim of arresting a big-time drug dealer. I was playing the big man, the man with the money, and I was keeping very quiet – that was my persona at the time. I was sitting in the back of the car with the baddie – the dealer. The driver was also a copper, there to look after me. While I was sitting there quietly, I left it to the driver to do most of the talking. Then the baddie said to him, 'Your mate don't talk much, does he?' To which he replied, 'No, he's a quiet one – he prefers to keep himself to himself.' The baddie turned to the driver suspiciously. 'So how do I know he's not a copper?' he said.

At this, my insides turned to jelly. There was absolutely nothing I could do, so I just tried to maintain my ice-cool exterior and calmly said to the driver, 'Tell him to get out the car,' referring to the baddie. He did, and we drove on. 'Fucking hell,' I said to my mate, 'that was a bit close!'

After about ten minutes, we went back and picked up the baddie, but I still didn't talk to him – I couldn't risk letting him know that we'd been spooked by his suspicion. Then my mate the driver said to him, 'You really upset him, you know? He really hates coppers.' The bloke went as white as a sheet and said, 'Oh, I'm so sorry!' He was seriously shaken up, and completely convinced by my little trick – and we got loads of gear from that job as a result. A huge quantity of cannabis, I think it was. And that's why I portrayed myself like that – being the quiet man was an effective strategy.

I'd been given my first undercover job way back in 1972 – the one that ended badly when I agreed to go to Kilburn to complete a drug deal, completely unaware that I was leaving my surveillance behind. I was the most experienced Black officer around at that point, so I was seen to fit the bill; I became the first Black undercover police officer. Even though the job didn't go according to plan, the powers that be can't have been too disappointed with me; I continued to be involved in various operations, eventually becoming one of the most experienced covert officers in the Met.

The way it worked was that I would receive a phone call whenever I was required, sometimes at incredibly short notice. I could get a call at 10 a.m., saying that I needed to be somewhere within four hours – it could be as quick as that. Some jobs lasted a single day, but other operations were more involved and could take me away from home for several days at a time. As the operator in the field, it was critical that I had the ability to pull out and withdraw at any point – that would be my decision to make.

Before you went on an undercover job, you had to be a little bit afraid of what might happen – if you went into a job blasé and confident that you were going to be the hero without any problems, you'd come unstuck. But the trick was to not let the criminals know what you were thinking. I can't say exactly how criminals work, because I'm not one of them, but one of the most important skills that was demanded by undercover work was the ability to figure out what you would do if you were in their position.

Primarily, they all want money. Once, I saw a bloke who was selling cocaine, and when he saw the money that he stood to make – £100,000 it was; a big suitcase of money – he literally started salivating and rubbing his crotch. It was clear that he couldn't stop himself from feeling a sort of primal urge when he saw what he thought he was going to get away with.

I'd always change my appearance, depending on the job – I mean, you wouldn't go into the Savoy dressed in jeans and a T-shirt, would you? So you'd buy your own gear – whatever you thought was suitable to help you fit in. You'd go to second-hand shops and buy cheap jewellery that made you look rich. I even got my ears pierced – two little piercings. When I was getting them done, the lady in the shop laughed at me because I was screaming like a child – I may have looked tough, but it bloody hurt!

Sometimes I'd wear dark glasses as part of my disguise – when I was wearing them, the baddies couldn't see my eyes, so I felt like they gave me an extra element of protection. I could be thinking anything, and they wouldn't have a clue. On other jobs, I wore ordinary glasses and sometimes I wore an eye patch.

It would be up to me how I turned myself out – feeling comfortable on a job was really important. But you'd have to dress appropriately, which meant fitting in with the people that you'd be mixing with and thinking about how they'd perceive you. They might think to themselves, *He's looking a bit too smart – he's got to be a copper.* Or, if you'd done a good job at fitting in, they'd think, *He looks a bit rough – he's all right.* My persona had to be someone that they respected, but I couldn't do anything to frighten them away.

I always went on a job prepared for the fact that the baddies might want to pat me down in case I was wearing a wire – I mean, I certainly would have done if I was in their position! I couldn't risk that happening, so I'd try to make myself a bit intimidating, but not so intimidating that I'd scare them off. I couldn't do anything that would made them think, *Fucking hell, I don't want to go near this geezer.* I had to be approachable but unapproachable at the same time – that was the trick.

In addition to having a persona when I worked undercover, I'd always operate with a pseudonym. My name would never be Norwell Roberts; it might be 'Joe Soap' or 'Dickie Bird'. The idea was that you made yourself someone who could disappear into thin air at any point, with no one having a clue who you were. By the time the baddies realised that they'd been caught out, I'd no longer be on the scene.

It was always a possibility that word would get around about you. After all, criminals would talk to each other – if any of them twigged that I was a copper, the game would be up. In order to avoid this, it was important that they never knew anything about me. I might tell them my name was Joseph. 'What do you do?' they might ask. 'Oh, a bit of this, a bit of that,' I'd reply. I might tell them that I'd done a bit of time, but it was crucial that I'd never tell them which prison I'd been in. If, for instance, I said, 'Yeah, I've done five years in Pentonville,' there was a chance that they'd have people in their gang who were in Pentonville, so they'd be able to find me out. So you'd leave it vague, while giving them enough information to trust you. By the end of a job, I'd know everything about them, but they'd know absolutely nothing about me. That was the art of undercover work.

The undercover work was only one part of my career, of course – after all, my main grounding was as a PC and then as a regular detective. But it was something I was asked to do, and I enjoyed it. Working in CID, I was already doing a sort of undercover work – you're in plain clothes rather than uniform – but I was thrilled when things got a bit more serious and I was chosen for a new undercover squad which operated out of Scotland Yard.

It was 1988 when a special operations unit dedicated to undercover work was formed, coordinated at a national level.

The intention was to bring together all the officers who had been operating independently and combine their knowledge and skills.

There were just twelve of us in the Covert Operations Group to start with – twelve of the most experienced undercover officers who had, until then, been carrying out covert operations in various police forces all over the country. The objectives of the unit would be to provide trained officers and resources for cases that required covert policing, and to help with evidence gathering where required.

The twelve of us were summoned to a meeting at Hendon, and we turned up in the types of outfits that we typically wore when we were working undercover and trying to look like villains. Although we might have seemed like a right motley bunch of every shape, size and colour, we were, in fact, an elite squad of undercover detectives – I was proud to be part of this illustrious group, and I was damn well going to make a success of it. As we walked from the classroom to the canteen, past the school's young uniformed recruits, you could just tell they were thinking, *What the hell are that weird bunch of blokes up to?*

The objective of the new unit was to develop a training package that could be used to teach officers how to work undercover. Role play formed an important part of the course; those of us who had a lot of experience would typically take on the role of a villain, which might mean a guy selling drugs, stolen watches or forged currency. Being aggressive and putting the trainees through mental stress was all part of the training – we needed to see how they'd cope when they were under pressure.

It was fascinating to watch the new undercover officers trying to learn the skills that the role demanded, and I relished teaching them how to act like the bad guy. We acted out lots of different scenarios, some of which involved planning what we would do if a job went terribly wrong, leading to us being exposed as a police officer and taken hostage. I knew from experience that even if I was taken as a hostage, I'd never admit to being a copper; doing so would mean putting other people at risk.

The course was very challenging, but that was the whole point; the aim was to work out what we would do in scenarios that were even more difficult than the ones that we would be facing in real life. I played many roles, and regularly found myself acting as a stooge in the hostage-negotiators course that was undertaken by senior officers. It was fun, but the standards were high and not everyone made the grade.

An undercover job could involve any crime where it was thought that the employment of a covert officer could achieve the best results. Scotland Yard knew I had the skills to work anywhere and among people from all walks of life – plus, as a Black undercover officer, I was in a tiny minority. Although my skin colour probably was an advantage at some points – there were so few Black police officers that I came under much less suspicion – I was never stereotyped and worked with all colours and creeds. After all, adaptability is one of the most important skills in the armoury of an undercover officer.

The first commendation I received for my undercover work was awarded for 'detective ability and professionalism resulting in the arrest of four men for conspiracy to supply cocaine and possession of cocaine with the intent to supply'. The job involved ensnaring a millionaire drugs baron, which meant posing as a gangster.

If the criminals were going to be convinced by my alter ego, I had to look the part. I was dressed in a suit with lots of gold jewellery – just what you'd expect. We sat in the car for an hour, waiting for the target, unaware that he was there the whole time. He was checking us out to see if he was being set up. There were surveillance people in the car park, but he didn't realise that.

Although I had plenty of backup, it was my job to get him to incriminate himself. Drug dealers who operate on this scale are especially paranoid, and everything depends on the first meeting. When you first meet them, you look at each other, aware that you're both thinking exactly the same thing: *Can I trust this man?* I was wearing a gold bracelet, and he said, 'Cor, I'd love that for my son.' So I replied, 'If this job comes off, I'll give it to you as a present when I come back to do the next one.'

Once I'd won his trust, I gradually built up a relationship with him, to the point where he felt safe enough to store the drugs at his own house. When the day of the deal finally came, armed police took him by complete surprise. They'd abseiled down the side of his house and bent the soil pipe; if he tried to flush the drugs down the toilet, he wouldn't be able to. The front door was reinforced; when they eventually got in, they seized fifty kilograms of cocaine – much more than they were expecting. The dealer was arrested, along with three accomplices – a job well done. As always, I was relieved to get home in one piece.

I don't think there's any question that undercover work is an effective form of policing, but the challenges that come with doing the work are enormous, and one of the most important qualities of a good undercover officer is the ability to thrive under the pressure. It's hard to replicate how it feels when you're on a job, with the adrenaline flowing through you, but I came to find it very addictive.

Before I started a job, I'd always be a bit apprehensive, but this was a good thing – I needed some adrenaline pumping through my veins to make me alert. Otherwise, I might find myself making a silly mistake. At this point I'd be wondering what the job was going to entail and what role I was going to have to play, but I'd only find that out at the briefing. I soon learned that no matter how much you plan an operation, it's never enough

– criminals are always unpredictable, so a lot of the skill lies in the ability to think on your feet.

This ability was tested by one particular job, when I found myself acting as driver for a gang of crooks planning to rob a warehouse. The idea was that by being involved in the raid, I could ensure that when they went through with it, there were uniformed officers ready to catch them. The job seemed simple enough.

There were three of them in the gang and they were dressed all in black and wearing balaclavas, but they were clearly nervous and I found myself sat in the car with them as they kept putting off the moment to strike – I started to wonder if they were going to go through with it at all. They kept taking the balaclavas off and putting them back on again. They were all tooled up, but they were just sitting there playing with their guns, winding them around their fingers and twirling them, just like cowboys used to in the Western films I'd loved so much as a kid. They were loading and unloading them, comparing weapons like they were toys and counting the bullets. While they were doing all this, I just sat in the driver's seat and did my best to remain calm, just as I'd been trained.

All of a sudden, a security guard came up to the car, wondering why we'd been parked up for so long. I wound the window down slightly – careful not to let him catch sight of my passengers – and he asked if I was OK. 'Yeah, mate – I'm fine thanks,' I said. 'I'm just waiting for someone.' I'd kept my cool, but my new mates seemed to be a bit spooked by the attention and we ended up waiting for another quarter of an hour as a result. While we sat there, I let them do most of the talking – the idea, as ever, was that I would get to know everything about them, but they would find out absolutely nothing about me. I occasionally chipped in, contributing the odd word to the conversation – it was important to keep them thinking that I was on their side – but as far as they were concerned, I was just the driver.

Eventually, they decided to go through with the job. All three of them ran towards the warehouse, while I waited in the car; to my huge relief, they didn't ever come back, a sign that everything had gone according to plan – they'd been nicked.

I was so stressed by what had happened on that job that I couldn't drive back to the police station – I was shaking too much. I'd been sat in the car for nearly four hours, and the whole time I'd been on edge, desperately hoping that they wouldn't twig and work out that I was a copper. My adrenaline levels had been so high for so long that when it was all over, I was left feeling completely drained.

I did undercover work for more than two decades, on and off. The frequency of jobs would vary from one month to the next; I might be summoned by Scotland Yard every six weeks or so, but it was very sporadic.

Sometimes, I'd take on a job that would end up coming to nothing – the bloke I was supposed to meet might not turn up and the job would be scrapped. Once or twice, I called off an operation myself. If something about the person I was going to meet made me feel uncomfortable or if a detail of the set-up wasn't quite right, I wouldn't go through with it – it wasn't worth the risk. It was crucial that I was completely happy with the situation; having messed up my first undercover job, I was determined not to make the wrong decision again.

I'm not able to put an exact number on the amount of crimes that were prevented or solved because of my work, but I can say for sure that there were plenty of arrests and a great deal of drugs and stolen goods were seized. I was happiest when I was working on my own, because other people generally added stress to the job – they were extra elements that could go wrong, but I'd sometimes find myself working in a pair or a trio. One of the trickiest things about working with other people was that you'd need to remember the details of your mates' alter egos as well as your own.

I was fortunate that there were never any disasters, but there was one occasion that came pretty close. I was on a job with another covert officer and we were sat in a vehicle, along with the baddies, having a conversation, when something terrible happened; my colleague had some kind of mental blank and inadvertently called me by my real nickname – Noz – rather than my pseudonym. It was a real bottle-tester; if such a moment were to occur in a Hollywood movie, there'd be dramatic music, with the camera panning between all the characters to observe their reactions. I showed no emotion and, fortunately, the baddies didn't twig – they were too busy thinking about the crime they were about to commit to notice what had happened. We just carried on talking, relieved to have got away with it.

I'm very lucky that I didn't ever work with anyone who ended up getting so involved in a case that they 'went native' and found themselves sympathising with the criminals, but you always had to be on guard for the possibility. Undercover work was completely different from what I did the rest of the time – there was no time to laugh and joke. I had a job to do, and if I was to return home without getting into trouble, I had to keep my wits about me at all times.

Obviously, there's no way that anyone could do this sort of undercover work twenty-four hours a day, seven days a week – the constant pressure would lead you to burn yourself out and have some sort of breakdown. Working in this way takes a lot of nerve and calmness under pressure, but the body can only handle so much of it; I've known lots of undercover officers who have ended up suffering from mental illness, and I did not want to join them.

In public, I've always said that my undercover work did not cause me any ill effects. However, even now, when I first enter a room or find myself in a public place, I automatically try to position myself in a corner where I can see everybody. If anybody jumps up on me suddenly, I find myself acting a bit defensively, but I think anyone who's been a police officer is probably prone to that sort of behaviour – it's force of habit!

When I was working undercover, no one knew – not even my wife. I didn't discuss the jobs with her at the time, because I wanted to protect her. Part of the reason for this secrecy was the knowledge that I wasn't only risking my own life – I could also be putting the lives of other people at risk. Make no mistake, there are some nasty people out there. And had they found out what I was doing, they would have had no hesitation in getting rid of me.

My colleagues at every station where I worked were also kept in the dark about my undercover work – all they would be told was that I was doing police business elsewhere. That could cause a lot of tension with my bosses – they thought they were in control of me, but I had to prioritise the demands of my governors at Scotland Yard. Once, one of my detective inspectors rang me up when I was on a job and said, 'When are you coming back to work?' I couldn't tell him anything – the fact was, I'd only be able to return to the station when the job was finished. He hated the fact that he had no control over me. I told him to fuck off and hung up the phone. He thought he was being clever and was trying to play with my mind. However, I was in my other role and was in no state to discuss my work rota!

The wife or partner of an undercover officer has to put up with a lot, but I was very lucky that I could always leave my work behind when I got home. I could be away on an undercover job for as long as a week and as far as Wendy was concerned, I was just at work – what she didn't know about, she didn't have to worry about. She might have noticed that I was dressed in some funny gear, but because she didn't ask any questions, I didn't have to lie to her. She'd see me going into work in the morning dressed up to the nines and I'd just say, 'I've got to go somewhere,' taking my little walking cane with me. When I went away, I'd always make sure that she was looked after at home – we're very lucky to have good neighbours and friends around us.

Given that I was involved in undercover work for some twenty-five years, I think I'm entitled to say that I was good at it! I'm confident that when I was dressed up as one of my alter egos, I could've walked past most of my friends without them recognising me. However, the disguises were just one aspect of how I kept myself safe while working undercover; another key element was the ability to change from one role to another. To put it another way, I had to be able to take on many characters, and to switch between them with ease.

For example, in any single undercover job, I'd think of myself as several different people. First, I was the person who went into work in the morning. Then the call would come through and I'd be requested for a undercover job; I'd have to get into that mode straight away, which meant going home to change my outfit. Then, when I got to the job, whether it was in Brighton, Scotland or Wales, I'd be a different person again. Finally, I'd be the person who had to debrief my colleagues on what had happened. Having finished the job, these various elements of my character returned to one and I'd be back where I started.

To be able to cope with all this, I constantly worked on my role-play skills, building on what I'd practised back at training school. I've often thought that the skill came easily to me because I saw it as acting – but the difference was that a poor performance during an undercover job could have far more serious consequences than a bad review!

I've been asked many times since my retirement why I'm still so secretive about what I did when I was working undercover. To put it simply, I always kept a single phrase in my head: 'Loose lips sink ships.' There are a few reasons why I'm reluctant to reveal too much information, but the main one is that I don't want to risk saying anything that might help the baddies – I know how hard it is to keep one step ahead of them, and I'd hate to do anything that risked jeopardising officers' work. It's a bit like talking to retired soldiers about what they did behind enemy lines during their military careers – most of them would not breathe a word about their experiences. Working undercover was far more stressful than day-to-day police work, and you can't imagine what it feels like if you haven't actually done it. In terms of whether it affects me today, I try not to spend my life looking over my shoulder, but I'm always aware of what's going on.

Overall, I enjoyed working undercover – it tested my detective ability and my acting. We put some bad guys behind bars and made society a safer place, and I often smiled to myself when I read newspaper reports covering cases that I'd worked on behind the scenes. I'd always said that I would know when it was the right time to stop undercover work, but I still regret the fact that I was forced to stop by a senior officer rather than of my own accord; as I'll explain later, I believe a bad decision was taken by a chief superintendent who bore a grudge against me, and that it risked the lives of two undercover officers.

20

A Stressful Time

THE YEARS ROLLED on as I worked in my day job and took on undercover work whenever I received a call. In 1988, it was time for me to leave Wembley and move to Barnet, an area that I knew nothing about – I'd never worked so far away from Central London. As always, arriving in a new area meant starting from scratch – the local knowledge that I'd built up in my last station would be of no use at my new one. It didn't matter to the powers that be where you lived – as a police officer in the Met, you'd serve wherever you were told. That could mean driving to the other side of London to get to work – as long as you could get there on time, that was all that mattered. They'd post you wherever, and if they wanted to take the piss, they would. You could be living in Buckinghamshire and end up being posted in Croydon!

I moved to North West London in 1976, quite early in my police career, and I've lived in the same house ever since. In a way, it's probably better not to work on the patch where you live – you might have to nick people you went to school with or even your neighbours. If you worked a long way from home, at least you could get away from work without being surrounded by it.

All I knew about Barnet before I was stationed there was that it was S Division, and that the call sign for the nick was 'SA'. The Barnet subdivision took in a chunk of countryside so big that I'd need a car to cover it. A few days before I was due to start, I drove there. Compared to what I was used to, there were a lot of fields and green space – it was the sort of landscape that I hadn't seen since my childhood days in Bromley. When I found the nick, I was surprised to discover that it was quite a new building – very different to any of the stations where I'd previously been posted.

Soon after I started there, I was asked to be the supervising officer on the crime desk. I embraced the challenge – having worked on the first crime desk back in 1977, I was certainly well qualified for the role! I was allowed to pick my own officers, and I made sure I chose carefully – I wanted a team of workers, not shirkers. My boss was Detective Chief Inspector Brian Cooper, who was approachable and a good listener, with the ability to make the right decisions and a calm, unflappable manner.

Very early on in my time at Barnet, there was a small sign that life there wasn't going to be easy. Every day, I'd take a packed lunch to work and place it in the fridge. During my first week, when I went to retrieve my lunch, it was nowhere to be seen – the only explanation was that one of my colleagues had eaten it. That evening, I came up with a plan to identify the culprit. I asked Wendy to make me a cheese omelette laced with a liberal sprinkling of finely chopped Scotch bonnet chili peppers. The next day, I placed it in the fridge as usual and waited to see what happened. When I spotted one of my fellow officers wiping his brow, drinking copious glasses of water and dashing to the toilet, I knew that I'd got my man! Needless to say, that was the last time anyone pinched my lunch.

It took a lot to shock me in those days, but during my time in Barnet I encountered a crime so cruel that I resolved to do something about it. In those days, artifice burglary usually occurred when a conman knocked on the front door of an elderly or vulnerable person, pretending to be a representative from the water or gas board. He would normally pretend to be investigating a leak or something similar, suggesting that there was a problem that posed a risk of serious damage. While one of the criminals was talking to the homeowner on their doorstep, another one would be pretending to check for damage, but he would actually be rooting around the property for cash or jewellery.

On one occasion, I was quoted in the local press as saying that the unsavoury characters who committed such crimes were 'scum'. As a result, I was hauled into the chief superintendent's office and told that I should not refer to criminals in this way – but as I made very clear during my dressing down, that was one of the kinder words I could have used! After a frank exchange of views, the chief superintendent reluctantly agreed that my choice of words was accurate, even if he wouldn't have used it himself. But then, I've always believed in calling a spade a spade!

One particularly cruel case of this type of fraud began when an elderly man and his wife were doing their weekly shopping on Whetstone High Road. The couple were approached by a man wearing a green boiler suit who told them he worked for the water board. They were completely taken in by his story – he made it clear that he knew where they lived and told them that his computer indicated that there was a serious leak in their home, before adding that someone would come to their home later that day to investigate.

Soon after the couple returned home, another man in a boiler suit came to their door – an accomplice of the first. He told them that he needed to inspect the house and pointed out two damp patches. The truth of the matter was that he'd hidden bags of water under his overalls, which he poured onto the floor when the couple were distracted.

He told the poor couple that he was going to have to call a specialist firm to fix the problem; the cost would be £3,400. When the couple offered to pay by cheque, he told them that this would only delay the work; if they paid in cash, the problem could be resolved immediately. The husband managed to withdraw the money from his bank and, as promised, the 'workman' turned up shortly afterwards and took all the money, before slipping out the house and making their escape when the couple's backs were turned.

Hearing about the suffering caused by this crime – in addition to countless similar stories – led me to launch a campaign. I was the police representative who had to liaise with the local press, and every week I found myself stressing the nastiness of this crime and urging the public to be careful when they answered their front doors. I emphasised that they should never allow anyone into their homes without checking their identities by contacting the relevant agencies. I realised that this was not always easy for an elderly person, but all the evidence suggested that if entry was thwarted, the thief would invariably just give up and look for an easier target.

I was reminded of the problems faced by victims who fell for this sort of scam when I asked one of them why she'd allowed a thief into her house so readily. She replied sharply, 'It's all right for you, Officer, but I haven't seen or spoken to anyone for a week.' From that moment on, I made it my business to spend some of my time helping the elderly, especially those who lived on their own.

The biggest challenge with tackling this sort of crime was educating the public about the steps they could take to protect themselves. The person committing the crime could be of any age – even some children, who looked as if butter wouldn't melt in their mouths, seized the opportunity to take advantage of the vulnerable. One common trick would be for two boys to knock on the front door of a house with a side gate and tell the occupant that their dog had gone astray and run into their back garden. The victim would then take one of the boys around the side of the property and into the garden, while the other boy would seize the opportunity to rifle through the house for valuables.

The youngest conmen I encountered during my career were a trio of nine-year-old boys who gained access to the homes of the elderly by asking for a glass of water or pretending to be desperate to use the toilet. They were eventually caught when one of their victims, an eighty-year-old woman, became suspicious and called the police. As the lads were under the age of criminal responsibility, they could not be charged and so were released into the care of social workers.

I was shocked by this type of crime, which seemed to be becoming increasingly common. We worked with the utility companies to ensure that all their employees were made to carry official ID. We also teamed up with the local MP to come up with a 'doorstep code', which was published in local newspapers and printed on leaflets that were posted through people's doors. At the top of it was the slogan 'If in doubt, keep them out!'

To this day, I'm proud to have been one of the instigators of this campaign, which did a great deal to protect some of the most vulnerable in society. The messages of congratulations that we received from various organisations and dignitaries were very welcome, but the letters of thanks from members of the public were even more special – even now, they are among the most treasured items in my scrapbooks.

Some years later, when I was working at Golders Green, I found myself investigating a similar sort of crime. An elderly lady had called the station nearly every day for years to complain about the theft of some valuable paintings. She'd ramble on without making much sense, but one day I decided to visit her at home and investigate her claims properly. My colleagues thought I was as mad as she was when I told them what I planned to do, but when I met her, I discovered that she was far from rambling – in fact, I was able to take enough details from her to follow up on her allegations. It turned out that a workman had tricked his way into her house and stolen two valuable paintings while her back was turned.

I was by now something of an authority about this sort of offence. After a lot of investigation, I was able to trace the paintings to a shop in The Lanes in Brighton, and then made sure that they were returned to their rightful owner. I wasn't able to trace the thieves, but the lady's calls to the station, which had been ignored for many years, stopped. This was a sober lesson to those police officers who had fobbed her off, and a reminder of what we were there to do.

I dealt with a huge variety of cases at Barnet, and some of them were very distressing. One of the most difficult was a case where a husband was stabbed by his wife after a row. It is usually women who are the victims of domestic abuse, of course – this was the first time I'd arrested a woman for assaulting her husband. Once we'd taken them both to the station, he became a 'hostile witness', refusing to press charges and to make a statement against his wife, so the case was discontinued.

That was an emotional case, but the ones that involved the abuse of children were even more difficult. During the investigation of sexual offences, especially when children are involved, it is crucial that police officers do not allow their personal feelings to interfere with the investigation. In the old days, police officers often used aggression as a tactic in interviews, but in my experience it does little except make suspects scared and less likely to assist with enquiries, while there's also a risk that it can lead to false confessions. I'd always been good at persuading people to cooperate, and I put my success down to the fact that I'd always try to get inside their head during an interview. I'd start off by asking myself what they would expect me to do next, and then I'd do the opposite.

If, for example, I found myself interviewing a man who was accused of indecently assaulting a young boy, I would always try to stay calm. This tactic would play havoc with the suspect's brain; he would probably have expected to get a good hiding in the cells, and so would be completely confused by the offer of a cup of tea or a cigarette. The fact that I was a big bloke helped, too – being gentle seemed out of character, which worked to my advantage.

Although I worked on plenty of interesting cases at Barnet, I found my time there difficult, thanks to a tricky relationship with my superiors – it felt like the jealousy that I'd been the victim of previously had once again begun to rear its ugly head. At this point, I'd been doing undercover work for some time, meaning that I'd take instructions from Scotland Yard. My boss at Barnet seemed to resent the fact that I could be whisked off to work elsewhere without warning, and it irritated him that I couldn't tell him anything about what I was doing and how long it would take. As a result, doing this work alongside my normal day-to-day duties became increasingly uncomfortable. I felt like I was caught in a trap, being pulled in opposite directions by my conflicting responsibilities. However, in any battle where Scotland Yard was involved, my local station was always going to have to settle for second place.

At some points during my time at Barnet, work got so stressful that I felt like chucking it all in and resigning. I dreaded having to go into work – I'd just about had enough. The only thing that kept me going was the fear of being seen as a wimp – I knew resigning because of stress would be regarded as a sign of weakness in those days.

Things got so bad that I began to suffer from stress eczema; an itchy rash appeared all over my body, spreading from my arms. I went to see my doctor, but the medication that he prescribed didn't make any difference. When I returned to his surgery, he admitted that he was at a loss as to the cause of my condition, but said that he would refer me to a dermatologist. Then he added, 'The only thing is, he's South African – do you mind being treated by him?' 'I couldn't give a toss where he comes from,' I replied, 'as long as he cures me!'

I went to see Dr Arun and we became firm friends – I had no idea what he thought about his country's apartheid regime, but we avoided the subject. One of the first questions he asked me was whether I was having any trouble at home. I told him that I wasn't, and then he asked whether I was having trouble at work; I gave the same answer. It was the truth as I saw it, but I would later realise that I'd programmed myself to think that – I'd suffered in silence for so many years, afraid to admit defeat, that I'd lost sight of the reality. The way I was treated in the police force had got under my skin and it was beginning to affect my physical health, but I still couldn't admit it.

Dr Arun asked me a few more questions, before suddenly asking for a second time, 'Are you sure you're not having trouble at work?' I found myself admitting something out loud. 'Well,' I said, 'there's a certain individual at work who's really giving me a hard time.' The doctor quickly said, 'Yes, I think that might be what's causing the problem. And if you could go back to work and throw him out of the window, I guess that would make you feel a lot better?'

This analogy made a lot of sense. I could see exactly what he meant – that if I no longer had to deal with this bloke, my life would be easier and a lot less stressful. I was beginning to feel better already – I suddenly knew what the problem was and could start to deal with it.

Then Dr Arun tried to give me a simple explanation. He said that stress has to come out somewhere, and in my case it was coming out via my skin. It was like it had been buried inside me, and the problems I'd been having with my supervisor were the straw that broke the camel's back. It hadn't happened at the start of my career, when I was under the most stress – in those days, I was able to go back to the section house and cry. The doctor prescribed me an ointment that I picked up from the chemist, and after a year or so I was able to see the results – while the prescription helped, I think having the cause of my condition identified made a bigger difference.

In 1989, I reached twenty-two years' service (including my two-year probationary period), a milestone in the police force. The Police Long Service and Good Conduct Medal was first awarded in 1951; for an officer to be eligible, the chief constable must recommend them to the Home Secretary, while certifying that they have served for the qualifying period as well as being of good character.

Together with a number of other officers, I was summoned to a ceremony at Hendon, where my police career had begun all the way back in 1967. I was the first Black recipient of the award. Wendy and her mum were there to cheer me on. Unfortunately, my own mum was not well enough to attend – she was experiencing the early stages of dementia and was too poorly. Her absence made me sad, as I knew how proud of me she would have been had she been well enough to be aware of the significance of the honour.

At the ceremony, I had the opportunity to meet some of the officers who had been in my class at Hendon in 1967. There were a few others who had joined on the same date as me, but for one reason or another had left the force without making it this far.

During his opening address, the commissioner ran through the various important events that took place in 1967, the year that all the people being recognised had joined the police force. My ears pricked up and I listened intently, hoping that he would mention the recruitment of the first Black officer in the history of the Met, but nothing. I was a little surprised that twenty-two years on, I was not deemed worthy of a mention – someone had dropped a clanger!

There was one other slightly embarrassing moment during the ceremony, which seemed to highlight the discrimination that I'd been fighting against for the previous two decades. As I was being handed my medal by the Commissioner of the Metropolitan Police, Sir Peter Imbert, the photographer realised that his camera – which was quite old-fashioned, with manual rather than automatic settings – had been set up to photograph white people. He hadn't realised that one of the recipients of an award was Black. There was a slightly uncomfortable and lengthy pause while he adjusted the lens, apologising quietly and explaining that no one had told him that I would be there. I laughed awkwardly, as did the commissioner, who felt the force of my handshake as my grip got tighter and tighter – I wanted to make sure that he would never forget me again!

There was a shortage of officers at Borehamwood Police Station in 1990, so I was seconded there to assist the CID and to run a crime desk. Things went well and I enjoyed the work, but when the time came to return to Barnet I was unhappy at the prospect of having to go back to work for a boss who took pleasure in toying with my feelings. It was time for me to move on, so I applied to join the Child Protection Unit, which was stationed at Kingsbury in the borough of Brent. I filled out an application form, submitted it through my dreaded chief inspector and waited for a response.

Four weeks after the closing date, I asked the chief inspector if he'd heard anything about my application and he said he hadn't. When I asked if there was any feedback for me, he laughed and pointed to my application form, which was still sitting on his desk. 'I didn't send it in,' he said. Perhaps it was his idea of a joke, but I couldn't help but think that he'd acted out of spite – he obviously didn't like me. Once again, it felt like the colour of my skin had left me disadvantaged in the job that I loved. It took me right back to the bad old days of 'One down, two to go.'

I knew that if I'd stayed in the room and asked him to explain his actions I could have ended up doing something that I later came to regret, so I simply turned on my heels and walked away. I was sad, of course, but as Mr Sinatra said, 'that's life' – you win some and you lose some. I did not know it then, but I would come out on top in the end.

I'm quite sure there was a racist element to the chief inspector's refusal to submit my application – it was always there. I think he also resented the fact that I couldn't tell him anything about my undercover work. Maybe it was a combination of the two. Anyway, the incident confirmed in my mind that I needed to leave Barnet – for my own sanity, if nothing else. I'd had enough.

I rang the area headquarters at Kingsbury and asked to speak to someone in charge. I was put through to a deputy assistant commissioner and told him what had happened, before saying that I wanted to work somewhere else. He knew me well enough to understand that I wouldn't have been so upset without good reason. In fact, this would be the only time in my whole career when I asked for a transfer – I hadn't even asked to be moved from Bow Street during my torrid first few years in the force. It just wasn't my style, but at this point I'd finally reached the end of my tether.

The deputy assistant commissioner assured me that he would sort out the situation. He was true to his word; a few weeks later, I was transferred to Golders Green, which is where I would end my police career. I have no doubt that had I stayed at Barnet, I would have ended up taking early retirement.

Upon my arrival at Golders Green in 1991, I was introduced to the detective chief inspector, a nice bloke called Jim

McGoohan – who I believe was the cousin of Patrick McGoohan, the actor most famous for starring in *The Prisoner*. I'd worked with Jim before, and it was good to see a friendly face. He showed me the report about me that had been sent on to him from Barnet, and which included some very unkind remarks. 'They didn't like you very much there, did they?' he said. 'No, I don't think they did,' I replied.

I had no time to get upset, as Jim told me that he didn't care what they'd said – he'd always found me a sound geezer when we'd worked together in the past, and would rely on his own knowledge rather than remarks that clearly had racist under-tones. It was obvious that my old colleagues at Barnet had intended to put the skids under my move to Golders Green by making disparaging remarks about me to my new guv'nors, but I put it down to jealously.

In fact, to make his feelings on the matter crystal clear, Jim tore up the report that had come from Barnet and shredded it in front of me. 'As far as I'm concerned, Norwell,' he said, 'your time at Golders Green is going to start with a blank canvas.' I've no doubt that he would have come down on me like a ton of bricks if I'd ever disappointed him, but there was no way that I was going to do that. I was grateful to him for realising that I had been the victim of a clash of personalities at Barnet and for being prepared to judge for himself without believing every-thing he was told.

Sadly, Jim's life would be cut short due to illness, but I've always been grateful to him for giving me the opportunity to prove that what my colleagues in Barnet wrote about me was a complete fabrication. He was a proper gent and treated every-one fairly, giving praise when it was due and a bollocking when it was deserved – I don't think you can ask for much more than that.

Soon after I moved to Golders Green, an incident reassured me that the officers at Barnet who disliked me were very much in the minority. An officer who came from up north was travelling back to London after spending a weekend with his family. He was pulled over by a traffic car on the M1 for speeding; when the police officers asked why he was in such a hurry, he told them that he was on his way to work at Golders Green Police Station. One of them asked what department he was in, to which he replied, 'I work on the crime desk with DS Norwell Roberts.'

'Why didn't you tell us that you knew Norwell?' they said. 'You'd better get a move on – he won't appreciate it if you're late. And please give him our regards.' They would have definitely nicked him if he hadn't been my colleague; knowing me seemed to carry some weight – with some people, at least!

It wasn't long before DCI McGoohan put me in charge of the crime desk, the role that typically goes to the most experienced sergeant in the district. I reasoned that I must have something going for me – after all, I'd held this responsibility at stations all over London. I think I was known to be a safe pair of hands, and no one could question my willingness to work hard.

Senior officers in the police force can be quick to criticise and slow to praise, but I hope I'm not being big-headed when I say that I think I perfected the art of giving both. I always found that if my staff were happy, it was reflected in the quality of their work. On more than one occasion, I had to deal with young officers who felt they were being picked on. I'd take them under my wing and talk to them in a way that made them feel valued, and in each case they went on to be good officers. It was easy for me, as I knew what they were going through – it took me back to my days as a young PC. The only difference was that when I'd gone through difficult times, I hadn't been able to talk to any of my superiors.

★   ★   ★

During my police career, I heard countless stories from old coppers who would brag about how they'd 'hauled someone over the counter'. This was what they would all say they'd done when they arrested someone who was creating a disturbance in a police station. I'd always wanted to do it, and I was able to achieve my ambition when a man came into Golders Green and was stroppy towards the staff on the front counter. They called for my assistance and I noticed right away that he was being verbally aggressive. I asked him to desist several times, on the second occasion warning him that he would be arrested if he did not. 'What the fuck are you going to arrest me for?' he asked aggressively. 'Disorderly behaviour in a police station,' I replied with some glee.

I have to admit that I was pleased when his unruly behaviour continued, as I finally got the chance to arrest someone for that much-discussed offence. After he'd been arrested, he quietened down as he was processed. We placed him in a cell, before releasing him with a formal caution the next morning. A couple of days later, he returned with a box of chocolates and apologised to the staff he had abused.

I like to think that I didn't ever lose my ability to do the job during my long career, so I was distressed when this was questioned; one day, a chief superintendent at Golders Green summoned me into his office and told me that he'd decided I would no longer be allowed to work undercover.

The excuse he gave was that I was 'too old', even though I was only in my late forties. He said that he had my best interests at heart, but if you ask me nothing could have been further from the truth – the real reason, I believe, was that he was acting out of spite after I had made him look foolish during a hostage negotiation training course. I had been the anonymous 'hostage taker' acting out a scenario; he was the senior officer being trained, and he'd tried to get the better of me. I'd been given carte blanche to say what I liked – the idea was that he would develop a rapport with me. So he rang me up and said, 'Who's that?' 'Why – who are you?' I replied. As a guv'nor, he wasn't used to being spoken to like that. He told me his name, to which I said, 'So, what do you want me to do – have a baby?' I put the phone down and he had to ring up again – there had to be dialogue. When he rang up again, I said, 'Oh, fucking you again.' It went on like this – he was supposed to be getting inside my mind, but I was getting inside his. Everyone was laughing, because I'd made him look silly, and he can't have liked it. He should have known that if he couldn't control the hostage taker in a role-play situation, he'd have no chance in real life.

Playing around, at one point I said, 'There's a freezer here. If you don't give me what I want, I'm going to put the hostage in it.' He told me I couldn't do that, so I did. I think it was at that point that everybody realised that this chief superintendent didn't have any control. I was an experienced undercover officer, and he didn't realise that I was trying to help him – you can't allow people who are incompetent to be put in that situation.

Had it been real life rather than a training exercise, it could have resulted in the hostage coming to serious harm. Instead of placating me, he had decided to confront me. Anyone with an ounce of sense should know that it's a bad idea to wind up a hostage taker, especially when a police officer has been kidnapped, as was the case in this role-play. The correct tactic would have been to get me to comply with his directions, but he only succeeded in winding me up, and I had no option but to place the hostage in a freezer.

The hostage was eventually released, a little cold but unharmed, after the course director intervened. When the exercise was over, I stood up in front of the class and said, 'I'm Detective Sergeant Norwell Roberts – I hope you've learned something.' That was the first time they'd seen me. Looking back, I can see that it was a time when I put the importance of the job before my own career – I refused to go along with the office politics and defer to my superior.

The whole business reflected badly on the chief superintendent – he might have been able to do a desk job, but he was clearly unable to diffuse a serious situation and to placate a violent kidnapper. I possessed the ability to think on my feet, whereas he was clearly unable to do so. He went back to his station and it seems obviously never forgot the incident, clearly bearing a grudge. And I may be wrong, but I don't think he was ever called to deal with a hostage situation – he just wasn't up to it.

When Scotland Yard next requested my assistance in an undercover job, the chief superintendent – clearly bearing a grudge, if you ask me – refused; the two undercover officers who ended up undertaking the operation without me were shot and seriously injured. If I'd been working with them, as was originally planned, I feel sure this wouldn't have happened. Luckily, the officers survived – had things gone even more badly wrong and they'd been murdered, I expect he would have had a lot of explaining to do.

21

Speaking Out

A s my police career had progressed in the 1980s, I gradually became more confident about confronting the racism that I'd encountered within the force. I was also frequently asked to give talks at courses that had been organised by the Home Office as part of a racial awareness programme – the police wanted everyone to think they were taking a proactive approach to their lack of diversity. They were a good innovation, but unfortunately some of the officers who attended were there for the wrong reasons – not because they recognised that racism was a problem in the Met, but because it allowed them to escape the daily grind of police work.

I would always start my talks by telling a few stories about what I experienced in the early days of my career. After I'd said my bit, there would generally be a deafening silence and I'd have to break the ice by gently encouraging someone in the audience to ask me a question. Generally, a few attendees would say they would learn from my experiences, but some of them would always be very obvious in showing that they thought the course was a complete waste of time. I suppose the Met's desire to educate its staff was a positive thing, but the average copper on the beat wasn't sufficiently open-minded to be in favour of diversity. These courses were a start, but there was still a long way to go.

I remember giving one such talk to the Senior Command Course at Bramshill, the elite police college in Hampshire that was attended by up-and-coming officers from all over the country. I'd gone to lecture a bunch of these high-flyers, who were all destined for high rank; after I'd given my talk about the treatment I received at Bow Street, one senior officer said to me, in a matter-of-fact way, 'Well, what did you expect it would be like? All new recruits have their challenges – you should've known that you'd be treated like that.'

The room fell absolutely silent – you could have heard a pin drop. I couldn't believe that a supposedly intelligent senior officer at the most prestigious police college in the country would make such a stupid, thoughtless and unkind statement. The problem was that these recruits might have been highly educated, but some of them were still very old fashioned in their thinking. I often noticed that officers who were fast-tracked were less streetwise and capable – all they knew had been learned from books, the academic side of things. They might have been clever, but they didn't have a Scooby about how to get on with the man on the street.

In answer to that insensitive question, the truth was that I'd had no idea what to expect at Bow Street because I hadn't suffered racism since school. Was I right to keep quiet, or should I have spoken out? Other people might think I should have blown the whistle on how I was treated, but I was in a no-win situation. If I'd told the truth, my life would have been made even more miserable. It was only by pretending that everything was OK that I was able to carry on.

Obviously, the fact that I was still encountering prejudice more than two decades later demonstrated the institutional racism that still permeated the senior ranks of the police force. My reply was concise and to the point: 'Every officer deserves to be given respect and equality of treatment.' The pompous trainee said nothing, but there was a lot of eye rolling and sighing from some of his peers – he was clearly not alone in his casual racism. Reflecting on what had happened later that evening, it occurred to me that his attitude had made my point for me – and more effectively than my words ever could. I hope the rest of the course altered his views, but I don't hold out too much hope!

I'd always finish my talks in the same way, offering the following advice: 'If you see or hear racism, do something about it. Don't stand there and accept it. Approach the person, speak to them and point out the error of their ways. Do not be part of the walk-on-by society, and don't participate in so-called "canteen culture".'

Through the late eighties and early nineties, things were starting to change, both in the UK and abroad. Three of the first Black British MPs were elected to the British parliament in 1987: Diane Abbott, Paul Boateng and Bernie Grant, all of whom represented London constituencies. After a few years when there had been widespread feelings of powerlessness among the Afro-Caribbean populations of cities including Bristol and Liverpool, as well as London, and occasional rioting in protest at oppressive policing, race relations began to get more harmonious.

In South Africa, the great Nelson Mandela was released from prison in 1990; apartheid legislation was repealed the following year, and in 1994 Mandela became president, following the first election in which citizens of all races were allowed to vote. In London at this time, the Met was gradually beginning to feel more diverse. On 26 September 1994, I attended the launch of the Black Police Association within the Metropolitan Police. It had been organised by Chief Inspector Ronald Hope, the first non-white police officer in the UK to be promoted to that rank. He had asked me to be a founding member of the organisation, and I was pleased to accept his invitation.

I knew Ron pretty well, having first met him when he was a trainee at Hendon in the early stages of his career and I was there for another course. Since then, he'd obtained a degree in race relations, paid for by the police. Given what I'd been through in my early days, he asked me to help him with his dissertation; I was pleased to give him some relevant newspaper cuttings and we had several discussions about the problems that existed in the force.

The event was introduced by the commissioner Sir Paul Condon, who addressed an audience of police officers, MPs, high commissioners from the Caribbean and representatives from various societies. My name was second on the guest list, immediately after Sir Paul's, which felt like a nice recognition of what I'd done to shed light on the issue.

Four years later, in 1998, the National Black Police Association was formed, but I'd retired by then. I was not involved on any other matters to do with the BPA, but I was pleased that it existed and hoped that I'd had some sort of influence. As I said in an interview when I was asked what I thought about modern-day anti-racist movements, 'I'm happy for others to stand on my shoulders.'

In 2002, I was approached by the press and asked to comment on the forced resignation of a trainee officer who had made racist comments to a fellow recruit at Hendon training school. I took the opportunity to explain how difficult things had been for me as a new recruit at Bow Street. It was good to see that the Met had finally woken up to the fact that racism existed in the force and was prepared – at last – to do something about it. When I was asked whether I thought they were doing enough, I replied, 'What is enough? It will only be enough when there's no racism at all, when everyone is treated equally and no one suffers for being the wrong colour.'

While the Met is now much more diverse than it was when I first joined, the truth is that until the police service has been able to get rid of the institutional racism that has long plagued it, there will still be a problem. I've always felt that the best way to deal with racism is from the inside; it was for this reason that I was disappointed by the 2008 decision of the London branch of the NBPA to call for a boycott of all recruitment drives for ethnic minorities, in addition to its newspaper advertisements that cited a 'hostile atmosphere where racism is allowed to spread'. I felt that this sort of militant action had the potential to do more harm than good; as I said in an interview with *The Sun* newspaper at the time, I was worried that such an approach had potential to bite them in the bum.

I appreciate that there are occasions of extreme provocation – after all, I experienced some of these myself – but I'm inclined to think that an equally extreme response is always likely to be counterproductive. In this case, my caution turned out to be well-placed; the NBPA had been calling for a boycott in response to the suspension of its chairman Ali Dizaei, a commander at Scotland Yard. They claimed that Dizaei, who was accused of framing an innocent man, had been victim of a vendetta; following a protracted period of squashed convictions, retrials and numerous appeals, he would be jailed for perverting the course of justice and misconduct in a public office.

22

Retirement and Recognition

EARLY ONE MORNING in the early 1990s, with my retirement not far away, I was driving to see my mum when I was flashed down by a police car. I'd noticed that it had been following me for a couple of miles – it stood out like a sore thumb in my rear-view mirror. I pulled into a layby and two policemen got out – one of them was tall and the other was short. The tall one had his fingers in his truncheon strap, which made him look like he was trying to do an impersonation of John Wayne. His leg kept on shaking and he seemed nervous. His short colleague was writing notes furiously.

'Name!' they shouted out in unison. 'Detective Sergeant Norwell Roberts,' I calmly replied. At this, the tall took his hand off his truncheon, while the short one dropped his notebook and pencil and fumbled around for them on the ground. I think they were so nervous that they would have got on the floor and polished my shoes had I asked them!

It soon became clear that they'd made an incorrect assumption about me. *What's a Black man doing driving a nice car?* they'd thought. I decided to take the opportunity to teach them a lesson and invited them to come and meet my mum – I wasn't expecting them to accept the invitation, but I was pleased when they did.

I drove to Catford with them following behind in their panda car, and they sat on my mum's sofa while she prepared a tray of tea and biscuits. I guessed that they didn't know many Black people, and I wanted them to learn the importance of treating everyone with respect and reserving judgement. I suppose, if I'm completely honest, I also had an ulterior motive; I thought my mum, who was quite elderly by this point, would feel safer in her house if she was on friendly terms with a couple of the policemen in the area.

In December 1995, a letter was delivered to my home address postmarked 'Immediate' and bearing a Home Office stamp. That, in itself, was not a surprise – during my career, I'd received lots of letters from grand addresses. However, when I opened the envelope and read the letter, I found myself having to take a deep breath. It was from the assistant undersecretary of state, and it simply stated, 'Her Majesty The Queen has been pleased to award you the Queen's Police Medal for Distinguished Service. The Home Secretary wishes me to convey to you his warm personal congratulations on this award.' I was in shock; nearly thirty years after one Home Secretary had congratulated me on joining the force, I'd received congratulations from another one!

My first thought was that it had to be a wind-up – after all, the Queen's Police Medal is one of the highest honours awarded to police officers for distinguished service, and it's usually only given to chief constables and other senior ranks. I couldn't believe that I would've been recognised in this way, but the news finally started to sink in when my name appeared in both the *London Gazette* and *The Times* on 30 December, along with the other recipients of New Year Honours – it was actually happening. I've no idea how it had been decided that I should receive the QPM – I guess someone must have recommended me, but I've never found out who.

A few days later I received the royal warrant that came with the award; to my knowledge, I was the first Black police officer to receive this honour. Dozens of letters of congratulations followed, from colleagues and friends, as well as people who I didn't know personally but were aware of what I'd achieved. I even received a letter from an assistant chief constable who'd followed my career with interest; I'd never met him, but he remarked that my 'professionalism and courage in the face of extreme danger has won you the respect and admiration of your colleagues'.

The following February, the police at the area headquarters in Kingsbury organised a reception for me, which was a nice gesture. And then, on 15 March 1996, I went to Buckingham Palace to receive my award from Prince Charles, taking Wendy and her mum as my guests. I wanted my own mum to be there too, of course, but sadly she was not well enough to make the journey.

I hadn't ever imagined that I'd be invited to Buckingham Palace, so getting the opportunity to go was up there with my wildest dreams. I hired a chauffeured limousine for the day; we drove through the gates and walked to a holding area, before being ushered into the room where honours are given. Prince Charles congratulated me and asked me a little bit about crime in Golders Green – I could tell he'd done his homework on my career. He finished our conversation by saying, 'We need more men like you.'

At this point, a thought struck me. Just before I'd been presented to the prince, I'd been told not to ask him any questions or make any comments, but I decided that I had to make the most of this opportunity – after all, you only get one chance. I realise that it was a bit cheeky, but I said to Prince Charles, 'Looking around, you could do with a few Black guardsmen as well!' He smiled graciously, and I looked up at the members of the household cavalry who were standing either side of him, each holding a sword and staring back at me. That was my cue to go. I gave a swift bow and retreated.

It may not have been quite what Prince Charles meant, but the police force does need more men like me – while diversity in the Met has increased, there need to be even more Black and

Asian officers if it is to be properly representative of society. I met the Prince of Wales for a second time a few years later, when we were both guests at a passing out parade at Hendon. I was touched that he remembered me from our first encounter, and we exchanged a few words.

The day of my investiture went by in a blur. I felt so proud – in many ways, it was the pinnacle of my career. The difficulties I'd experienced during my early years in the force were a distant memory – being honoured in this way seemed to make every-thing I'd been through worthwhile. A photographer took lots of pictures that were released to the media and I was interviewed by various journalists. Once it was all over, we drove around in the limo, visiting a few friends to thank them for their support. One of them was Chris Ruocco, the legendary tailor who has a shop in Kentish Town. He'd kitted me out with the shirt, ruffs, top hat, tails and trousers that I wore to the palace – a very kind gesture, and I remain friends with him to this day.

It seems amazing, looking back, that I'd achieved so much by the time I turned fifty. When I reached this momentous birth-day, I wanted to mark the occasion with something special. Wendy spotted an advert for the perfect celebration: a weekend break on 'land, sea and air', travelling first class on all three legs. It would be one of the most memorable experiences of my life.

Our holiday began when we boarded the Orient Express at Victoria Station and travelled to Southampton, a waiter wearing a tuxedo serving us smoked salmon as we sped through the English countryside. We then transferred to the QE2 and sailed to Stavanger in Norway. The ship was as grand as you'd expect – we even had our own butler! When it was time for dinner, there was plenty on the menu that we liked, but Wendy fancied a Dover sole and the chef was happy to oblige. I swear that they must have thrown a line over the side especially! I ate caviar, which was served with toast and ice-cold vodka – delicious. I also happen to let slip that it was going to be Wendy's birthday a few days later. I thought nothing of it, but at the end of the meal we were surprised with a special birthday cake.

The weekend's pièce de résistance was a flight on Concorde. We boarded at Stavanger at noon and landed at Heathrow exactly an hour later, having travelled at twice the speed of sound. It felt like we were flying on the edge of space, but you'd never have known inside the plane that we were travelling so fast – it was so quiet and peaceful in the cabin.

The whole weekend was magical – a once-in-a-lifetime experience. And, of course, it can never be repeated – the QE2 is now a floating hotel in Dubai, while Concorde ceased operations in 2003.

A couple of years later, in 1997, I started planning for my departure from the police force. I was still only in my early fifties, but I'd served for thirty years, which meant my retirement was due. Once the word got out that I was calling it a day, I started to receive messages from well-wishers who lived all over the world. The interest was so great that someone even created a website all about the event!

I decided to throw a party to mark my retirement, but I was determined to foot the bill myself. I didn't want any collections to be made on my behalf – I'd seen how reluctant officers could be to contribute to the cost of other people's parties. A good friend called John Armstrong took on the responsibility of organising the event. I invited about 600 people, including the then police commissioner Sir Paul Condon, whom I had trained alongside at Hendon. Some of my colleagues from my first years at Bow Street were also there, but we managed to avoid talking too much about those early days – after all, I wanted it to be a positive event and had no desire to harbour any grudges.

I entered the party to the sound of bagpipes, and a jazz band provided entertainment during the evening. There was also a buffet and a very impressive cake. Sir Paul gave a speech and presented me with my Certificate of Service Award, along with a letter thanking me for everything I'd done for the Met. There was also a speech from the retired chief superintendent at Golders Green, Peter Twist, a man for whom I have a great deal of respect.

When my last day at work finally arrived, the press turned up in their droves and I gave countless interviews, which resulted in lots more press cuttings for my scrapbooks. One of my strongest memories of the day was being filmed for the national television news walking out of the police station for the last time. All the attention contributed to a feeling that I was leaving the force in the same way that I had arrived – with a blaze of publicity. However, I was happy with what I'd achieved during my career: I think I've changed some people's minds about Black people, won the respect of my colleagues and the public and helped to create a more diverse police force for those who followed in my footsteps.

Once I'd retired, I remained convinced that I had something to give, so I was pleased to be summoned to see Paul Condon at New Scotland Yard. 'Have you given any thought to what you want to do when you leave?' he asked. I told him that I'd seen some of the kids who were arriving in the force from the training school and wasn't very impressed with what they were being taught. 'I think I can educate them,' I said, upon which Sir Paul suggested that perhaps they should look at a role for me at the academy. But it came to nothing. I guess the police force is always moving on, meaning that us oldies are no longer required! I still think it would have been a good idea.

Since my retirement, I've remained active within my local community, spending a lot of time helping my neighbours and visiting the elderly. I've even been known to read to my ninety-four-year-old neighbour from her favourite Mills & Boon romance novels. I try to put my own slant on the stories, which makes her laugh. It's a lovely sight; if you've ever seen a ninety-four-year-old lady with tears of laughter rolling down her face, you'll know what I mean!

Another way that I've helped in the community is by giving presentations in schools on how I dealt with racism during my police career. I'm keen to get my message across to future generations, and letting them hear about the impact of racism firsthand is an effective way of doing this. We live in a multicultural society, and it's vital that Black history isn't regarded as separate; furthermore, it should be remembered all the time – not just during one month of each year. Until we reach genuine equality, we must do everything possible to celebrate the contribution Black people have made to society. It's good that we teach Black history so that others can be made aware of the difficulties and achievements of Black people in the past – in order to see how far we have come, we need to revisit the past, however uncomfortable that is. This is something I keep in mind when I visit schools during Black History Month. In 2017, after I visited a local primary school, I received a number of essays written by the children about my life and achievements. It was touching to see young people understanding the message of my presentation.

I've participated in eight Metropolitan Police Black History Month campaigns since my retirement – most recently in 2020, when the campaign was headlined 'A Voice for Change'. My photo featured in the publicity that was released on social media, in addition to posters on London buses and the Tube. And thanks to press interviews, I once again ended up seeing my face in the media as often as in the mirror! It seemed fitting that one of the interviews was conducted by the great Trevor McDonald; he, of course, had broken barriers in his own industry, most notably when he became the first Black news reporter on British television in 1973.

Having already been to Buckingham Palace to collect my Queen's Police Medal, I didn't think I'd ever get to go again. However, in

February 2007, a letter arrived from the Lord Lieutenant, inviting me to attend a garden party hosted by the Queen. This was followed by an official invitation from the Lord Chamberlain, and on 10 July, Wendy and I returned to the palace.

For this visit, I hired a chauffeur-driven black Bentley. We parked in Green Park and walked the short distance to the palace. Thankfully, it was a lovely sunny day – the event continues through rain or shine. I ended up chatting to one of the security officers, who by complete coincidence was a bloke called Alan Spencer, who I'd worked with at Golders Green. It was a good experience, and definitely something to cross off the bucket list!

In October 2016, I was invited by the chief superintendent of Hendon training school to visit the brand new Peel Centre. The Met had decided to name a training room there after me, in honour of my achievements – the first time a room had been named after a living police officer. The dedication ceremony for 'The Norwell Roberts QPM Training Room' took place in the morning, and in the afternoon I attended the passing out parade of 234 new recruits, as they marched to the band of the Queens Division.

While I was at Golders Green I'd received a letter from a lady called Mrs Blackett. Her husband had been an artist who liked to paint events from the news, and two of his paintings were of me. He had sadly passed away, but she was writing to say that she thought he would have liked me to have them.

I travelled to see her in Eltham, South London; she gave me the paintings and I gave her a charitable donation in return. I displayed one of them on a wall at home, and later decided to give the larger one to the training school in Hendon, where it is displayed in the training room that bears my name. Not bad for a poor Black kid who refused to succumb to the bullies!

Epilogue

T HERE'S A CHAP who's in the same Masonic lodge as me –
he's about my age and we get on well. I said to him recently,
'I bet you'd have been one of those officers who gave me a hard
time when I joined the Met.' He didn't say anything at first – he
just stood there mulling it over. And then he said quietly, 'Yes, I
probably would have.' I appreciated his honesty.

Not many people I know nowadays know very much about
my career. Masonry is a big part of my life, but in the lodge you
don't tell people a lot of detail about your background. I think
it's strange, in a way, that sometimes you only find out about
people once they've died, in their eulogy. You could sit next to
someone without knowing very much about them. For instance,
people I know might have read a bit about me, but most of them
don't take much notice. A few people have said, 'Oh, it sounds
like you had a rough time', without thinking much of it, but
then, when I've told the same people a little about my experiences, they've been in tears.

Even though I want to convey how bad things were, I never
want anyone to feel sorry for me. That's not my aim – I just
want them to know what I went through. People say, 'We didn't
realise – good on you for being so strong', but they don't realise
that I didn't think I was doing anything special at the time – all
I knew was that I wasn't going to let the bullies beat me.

In November 2016, I received a CA Legend Award, in recognition of my dedication to the Black community and in paving

the way for the next generation. When I went on stage to collect the award at the Hilton Hotel in Tower Bridge, I was lost for words – a rare moment! However, once I'd gathered my thoughts, I made the point that when I'd been at Hendon training school just a few months before, I'd been overwhelmed by the number of Black and Asian officers who had thanked me for paving the way for them. It had not been easy, but I had proved that everyone can achieve whatever they want, through determination in the face of adversity. I'm so happy when I see how many Black coppers there are on the beat these days – about time too!

During the recent Covid-19 pandemic, many of us were confined to our homes and suffered in ways that we could not previously have imagined. However, as a Freemason, I found myself able to put into practice something that I've learned over the years; how to care for people.

Every day, I make ten to fifteen phone calls, starting at around 7.30 a.m. On a single day at the height of the pandemic, I would make as many as thirty. Most of these calls are to elderly people who welcome a friendly voice asking them how they are – they tend to prefer a call, as they have not generally mastered the internet! I'm happy to spare someone five to ten minutes each day, knowing that it will make their life a little easier and bring a smile to their faces. I like to think that I'm a good listener, which is a skill that was especially appreciated during the various coronavirus lockdowns. When I heard about one old chap who had not left his house for several months, I made giving him a call part of my daily routine.

During these difficult times, when the police are so overstretched, it falls upon each of us to do our bit. As I know only too well, the police have a difficult job to do at the best of times, and it is through employing tact and good humour that they have most chance of encouraging people to comply with their directions. That was, after all, a lesson that I learned in my first week in training school. It worked for me then, and I see no reason why it can't be employed now. However, it is clearly a lesson that not all police officers are taught.

Since my retirement, I try to go for a walk every day, very early in the morning. Even now, I only need three hours' sleep a night, so I tend to get up at about 3 a.m. – and that's when I take my walks. I'm mindful of the dangers lurking in the surrounding streets, but sometimes they come from unlikely quarters. I've been stopped by officers in patrol cars on several occasions, which given the time of day I guess is not unreasonable. However, on one particular occasion in 2009, I was stopped by an area car containing two officers. The interaction started badly because of their attitude, and it went downhill from there.

The car pulled up alongside me and one of the officers said aggressively, 'Oi, what are you doing round here?' I replied that I was just out for a walk, to which he replied, 'We get a lot of burglaries around here, you know.'

I replied, 'Well, I live just down the road.' I was barely a hundred yards from the house where I'd lived for thirty-three years, since before the officers were even a twinkle in their mothers' eyes.

His aggressive tone continued. 'What's your name?' he said.

'Norwell Roberts,' I replied, and when he started to write it down, I added, 'Oh, don't forget to add the letters QPM.'

'What's that?' he asked.

'It's the Queen's Police Medal for Distinguished Service,' I said, and this is where things began to go wrong.

'Where did you get that from?' he asked. 'Did you get it on eBay?' I have to say that I bristled at this stupid remark; incensed at his ignorance, I turned on my heels and walked away.

If a police officer is polite at the start of an encounter with a member of the public, that will encourage the person they have stopped to be polite, too. The simple fact was that this officer's attitude had left a lot to be desired. After they'd driven off, I walked home and couldn't stop thinking about how badly he had treated me.

I decided to contact the local press about the incident, and the story made the front page – I didn't like the way I'd been treated and thought that speaking out would be a more effective way of highlighting the problem than making a complaint. I wasn't trying to castigate the officers, but I wanted them to realise that that if they expected assistance from members of the public, they had to treat them with respect.

Although the local chief superintendent took note of my comments and agreed that his officers should speak to the public politely, he went on to say he did not blame the officers for not knowing what the QPM was. 'Young police officers,' he said, 'might not be familiar with the honour.'

The local paper suggested that I might visit my local police station and give them the benefit of my knowledge on the subject, but I politely declined. After all, the correct course of action was for officers to be properly trained at Hendon and then at their stations – it was not my responsibility.

What probably happens is that officers are properly trained at the academy but then pick up bad habits when they are posted to their stations. Even now, police cars drive past me when I'm on my early morning walk. It would be nice if they wound down their windows to say good morning and perhaps stopped to chat for a couple of minutes, but they never do. Perhaps this aspect of their training needs to be adjusted.

In 2020, the murder of George Floyd by a police officer in Minneapolis sparked a debate on race relations and caused people all over the world to question whether they were doing enough to make society equal for everyone. While we are still clearly a long way from complete racial equality, I often find myself disagreeing with those people who say that Britain is as racist as ever – after all, anyone who says that probably has no idea how bad it was to live as a Black person in Bromley in the fifties and sixties, never mind South Africa or the Deep South of the United States. I know things are far from perfect and that there remains a lot of work to be done – we don't get it right all the time, but I think modern Britain is generally fair. Things have definitely improved since I first came here from Anguilla; and we've come a long, long way since the days when I was the only Black boy at school, or since I walked into Bow Street Police Station. When I think about those first three years, I now realise that I endured a systematic and unrelenting campaign of racial abuse. But despite that, I'm still grateful to those who gave me the opportunity to join in the first place.

The racism that does continue to exist will take time to be eradicated, and will be removed through education. I'll continue to tell my story for as long as I'm able. We have to work hard for a better future for the younger generation, in the hope that they will treat each other as equals, regardless of colour, class, gender and sexual orientation. We all need to respect and be kind to one another, and to do all we can to be positive role models within society. I've always tried to tread the right path in life, and I like to think that I've got it just about right.

Sometimes I think it's my own fault because I didn't show my pain – but I couldn't let them see I was affected. I now wish I'd confronted it, but back then I knew I couldn't. These days, it would be exposed in the press. Some people might think I didn't shout loud enough early on, but there was no one to shout to. Anyway, you can't fight something from the outside – I'd rather get inside and sort something from there.

In my Bow Street days, I was only able to cope by compart-mentalising things, separating work from home. Wendy has been by my side for forty-odd years, but I couldn't tell her about things that I talk about quite freely now – if I had, she'd have been worried sick every time I went to work. She knows about what happened at Bow Street now, but the first time she knew about it was when she saw it in the papers.

I wish I could take people back there and show them what it was like to walk down the street and have people shouting 'Oi, nigger' or 'Oi, Sambo!' at you. I remember talking to a bloke once, and he said, 'Me and my wife, we don't like Black people.' I said, 'How many Black people have you ever met?' He said, 'None – but I guess you seem all right.' It was clear that he was just afraid of people who were different to him, but once he realised that there was nothing about me to be afraid of, he was fine. That's what so much of racism comes down to – fear.

Various articles have been written about where I fit into the history books, and it has not escaped my attention that certain individuals seem keen to demean my achievements. I have never denied that John Kent became the first Black policeman in Britain in 1837, or that a mixed-race policeman called Robert Branford rose to the rank of superintendent in the nineteenth century. In my opinion, the debate around who was 'the first' matters far less than the question of whether others were able to follow in their footsteps. Unfortunately, Kent and Branford were forgotten about because no one came after them. It might have looked for a while as if I was going to be on my own for the long haul, but others were soon accepted; we now have many Black and minority policemen and women, some of whom have attained high ranks. Long may that continue.

I was hugely touched when Michael Fuller, the first ethnic minority chief constable in the UK, recently wrote about me: 'It was seeing a picture of Norwell that persuaded me to join the police. He was a great role model. Despite having such a tough time, he kept his dignity.' He went on to thank me and to say that, as a trailblazer, I'd showed what's possible and what can be achieved against the odds. It's very nice to hear someone who has achieved as much as Michael say something like that.

I do not seek to undermine the achievements of those who came after me. As I've said many times, I was not interested in being the first anything – all I ever wanted was to be a policeman and to get on with my job without suffering abuse.

Anyway, I hope my achievements stand on their own merit. If I've inspired just one person during my career, everything will have been worth it. How others view me is up to them, but I know one thing for sure: I am Norwell Roberts QPM!

Acknowledgements

There are too many to mention, but I would like to give a special thank you to the following people, past and present, without whom there would be no story:

My mum
Wendy Roberts
Alan and Sis Green & family
Nan & Grandad Miller
Rose, Barry, Michelle & Nicky
Edith Le Pers
The Cole family
Uncle Ernie, Auntie Eva & Marlene
Graham, Wendy & Abigail Clarke
Tony Carne & all at Revelation Films
Nick Humphrey
Kate Evans
Robert Asser
Professor Tony Fogg, John Burns & my colleagues at Westfield College
The Home Office police selection board

Marylands Day Nursery
Warwick Day Nursery
Jonathan Nicholls
John Armstrong
Brian Cooper
Richard Wells
Wendy Davenport
Nick Marshall
Peter Twist
Jamie
Pedro
Cheryl
All those people who worked with me on nine different crime desks
The community of Covent Garden
Elsie & Will Vandervelde from Broad Court
Brian & Maria
Blondie Mick

The kids from The Peabody
· buildings
David Stevens
Michael Whiting
The porters at Covent Garden
Market
Harry Pearce
John Rogers
Chris Ruocco
Pat & Breege
Noel & Tricia
David & Pam Dutton
All the people I've met in
Freemasonry
Bill Mills
Peter Baikie
Len Mellows
Richard Singh
Roy Sawh
Palo & Joe Singh
Alan Palmer
Norma Morgan
The TDC Class of 1972
Peter
Finlay Tinker
Dave Richards
Gary Numan
Ernie Neighbour
Ann & Bruno Deluca
Neil Birchenough
Dr Hamssa Mansour

Alan Davis
Bob Broeder
The Halac family
Dr Golden
Dr Abu
Dr Creighton
Dr Arun
The Commercial Attaché at
the South African Embassy,
1970
Roy Downard
Tony Moore
The Pearly King & Queen of
Acton
Roger & Stella Cowley
Michael & Carole Fahey
Jonathan Jones
Jean & Adele Graham
Mr & Mrs Cullen
Mr & Mrs Jaquest
Brigadier Bill Mills
Derek Caple
Derek Johnson
Gerald & Monica Lansley
Peter & Frankie Gilbert
The elderly lady who talked
to me while I was on point
duty on the Strand
John Ruth
My neighbours and local
friends